30

ONE-UPMANSHIP
(B.3)*

* "B" stands for Bottingham, a little-known collector of plant-galls, who achieved fame by using his knowledge of the techniques of botanical classifications to put order into the chaos of the Founder's many Lifemanship publications. According to Bottingham, One-Upmanship, 1952, is Number Three in the Gameslife series [1947 Gamesmanship (B1); 1950 Lifemanship (B2)].

ONE-UPMANSHIP

by

STEPHEN POTTER

———

BEING SOME

ACCOUNT

OF THE

Activities and Teaching

OF THE

𝕷𝖎𝖋𝖊𝖒𝖆𝖓𝖘𝖍𝖎𝖕

CORRESPONDENCE COLLEGE

OF

ONE-UPNESS

AND

GAMESLIFEMASTERY

━━━━━━━

ILLUSTRATED BY LT.-COL. FRANK WILSON

RUPERT HART-DAVIS
36 SOHO SQUARE LONDON W1
1952

PRINTED AND BOUND IN ENGLAND BY
HAZELL WATSON AND VINEY LTD
AYLESBURY AND LONDON

TO
ANDREW
AND
JULIAN

CONTENTS

PART ONE: THE COLLEGE

CONTENTS

CONTENTS

ACKNOWLEDGMENTS

I have indicated in the text my debt to the work and help of Lifestudents the world over in the preparation of this somewhat more ambitious and certainly more difficult volume. My grateful thanks are also due to the Editors of the following publications for permission to reprint portions of this work which first appeared in their pages: *The Atlantic Monthly, The Reporter, Punch, Vogue, Harper's Bazaar, The Lancet.*

S. P.

Regent's Park—Vicenza—Aldeburgh, 1949–52.

PART ONE

I

OUR COLLEGE

I AM SPEAKING to you now[1] as newly elected President of the Lifemanship Correspondence College. When I look at the list of distinguished names among our helpers and founders here I am astonished and even bewildered at the honour. Ours is a small community, housed quite modestly in a converted section of a converted mansion, yet from the files and the classrooms, the laboratories and the libraries, Lifemanship throws its lifeline from Alaska in the West to Colchester in the East.[2] Linked by vast sea routes,[3] it has been said of Lifemanship that we have been called into being in the role of the Old World redressing the balance of the New World redressing the balance of the Old.[4]

[1] These opening words form part of a lecture first delivered to a very small group in the waiting-room of Marks Tey Railway Station in January 1952. I am indebted to Sir Ford Boulder, chairman of the catering division of the Great Eastern, as it once was, for not withholding permission to print them here.

[2] There is as yet no Games-Life Association at Frinton, for instance, where one would expect it. Although a happy and natural result of the Aldeburgh Festival has been the founding of a small Lifemanship Club in that resort, it may be said that the Games-Life median line coincides unexpectedly with a Longitude which involves the tip of Cape Cod, famed in Melville.

[3] It is estimated that eleven-twelfths of Lifemanship's vast "Empire" is covered by water.

[4] But see pp. 152 ff (Hands-across-the-Seamanship).

13

But let me tell you something of our small self-contained University, not a thousand miles from Yeovil. Students from Wyoming, it is true, cannot reach us here. With them we deal, inevitably, by letter. For such, Correspondence College it must be; yet we prefer and welcome the personal touch, the human problem in the flesh; we are proud of the young lads and lasses who come to "L.C.C." to study at first hand.

We boast no domes or pediments. In spite of Gamesmanship Rallies and GIVE FREELY TO LIFEMANSHIP weeks, our dream of a worthy Senate House, built in Re-inforced Functional Revival, waits fulfilment.[1] Every penny of our endowment is spent on equipment, and it is spent on staff.

I should like to describe to you our workrooms— yes and our playrooms as well, not unlike those of one of the older universities, with whom we co-exist in mutual evaluation and respect.

Here a room which belongs to the Arts Faculty, at first like any other such; but look again and see how, in a detail, Lifemanship's doctrine of One-Upness is always followed or imbued. Note the piano with cigarette stains on the upper notes. But these are dummy surfaces removable at will, because it is not in all company that such signs of Bohemian inconsequence impress.

There is the conductor's baton—but where is the orchestra? In the gramophone cabinet, for it is the

[1] We are still without the government grant due to our foundation.

conducting of gramophone records which we teach, splendid way to corner attention and cause confused irritation when music is being played.

Look, too, at the wall devoted to pictures. But how are they arranged? "O.K." in gold letters denotes "O.K. to praise this year." On the right, in black, "Ex-O.K."—pictures which were O.K. ten years ago and which students must learn therefore to discard, for one-upness in pictureship.

See, too, our modern languages department. See our list of French phrases O.K. to bring into conversation. See, on the left of the blackboard, correct French; on the right, French translated into English French, phonetically transcribed, a dialect which

Fig. 1. Thinking in French (a Language Lifegambit).

During a ramble by the canal after one of our language tutorials, Cogg-Willoughby set us all laughing with this sketch of himself. "Some day you will see yourself in print," I said to Cogg. And here he is!

FIG. 2. "681 STATION ROAD."

Note in this recent drawing (A) dummy television aerial, (B) Founder's bedroom, (C) dining-hall with separate tables, (D) eucalyptus tree planted by former member of staff, Miss C. Johnson,

(E) eucalyptus tree planted by Founder, (F) sheer rock for Rockmanship, (G) ordinary putting-green, (H) lawn-tennis court (Vicarage
type), (J) museum of Clothesmanship (presented by the Harvard
Foundation and Mellon Trust), (K) dummy conservatory.

our students are taught to cultivate with aristocratic downrightness and amusingly insular don't-care-a-damnmanship.

Here, on this white tablecloth made of india-rubber, coffee-spilling is taught in our Mannership cadre, with demonstrations of how to apologise, or not to, and how, alternatively, to engineer, as host, the awkward pause and the "Don't-give-it-another-thought" sequence. (Lydall's[1] Reproach.)

In the Gamesmanship section, take a glimpse, now. That strangely shaped racket is a tennis racket, for use in study or office where Royal tennis strokes may be demonstrated to players who are merely lawn.

And why the two lawn-tennis courts? Note that A (left) is humpy, wobbly, the net sagging and stringy, tied to unsuitable sticks. On the right (B) all is taut and accurate, a Wimbledonship atmosphere, with all-steel umpire's chair and chromium seats for linesmen. It is here that lawn-tennis gambits *interchangeably suited to the contrasted gamesacre and lifeclimate of the two different courts* are worked out in detail. On this adjoining putting-green, the now famous intimidation plays and distraction gambits for putters were first taught to men who have since won success in this field on courses as far removed as Studland or Little Canaan. Nearby, in that asphalt corner, see stacked the rubber rapiers of our fencers with the special "BRUZELESS" boxing-gloves for students who need to say of this sport, too, in later life, "I

[1] E. (not J. B. C. W.).

18

once did a bit of it."
That sheer four foot of
plaster rock is for the
rockman (see p. 122)—
the mattress under-
neath is pneumatic and
shockproof.

The seeming shed be-
yond is in fact the
Museum of Clothes-
manship, with "Right"
and the equally Life-
manlike and gambitous
"Wrong" clothes stand-
ing adjacent for amuse-
ment and instruction.

Fig. 3. Museum of Clothesmanship.

For landing in Nairobi. Wrong
(left) and right (right).

Right and Wrong for grouse-shooting, for visiting
a coal mine, for the Tate Gallery, for New Year's
Eve, for landing in Nairobi.[1] And then, of course,
I would show you the College Dining-hall, the
Anti-social room, and the Library, with its dummy
books.

I want the pages which follow to be regarded as an
introduction to Correspondence College techniques.
It may be asked—why am I revealing all this? But
we are not a money-making concern—primarily. If
students are attracted by this glimpse of our methods,
we shall welcome them. If not, let them admit that
Lifemanship is not for them. I have seen some

[1] Oh, and countless others.

FIG. 4. A CORNER IN THE LIBRARY.

Note here the new student (H) breaking finger-nails on dummy books. *How will he deal with this situation?* Note desk with signatures of former students. Note empty bust-case. *One day it might be You.* On the left, genuine books. (D) *Gamesmanship* and *Lifemanship.* (F) The complete works of all nineteenth-century novelists in six volumes (shortened). (G) Classic French literature (abbreviated and epitomised for easy reading).

parents ruin many a natural Lifeboy by trying to force our philosophy on him when, at six or seven, he was too young, or too obstinate, to receive it.

Nor will I have it said that there is any mystery about ordinary Lifemanship, even if for obvious reasons its more advanced methods are known to initiates only. There are, of course, certain Super-gambits known only to Yeovil, and though we are in full and free consultation with Washington and the Pentagon on the possibilities of their exploitation, the technique of these is still our secret. Therefore it is, I suppose, not surprising that at the time of going to press the newspapers are full of an incident for which some will revile us, though others have shown sympathy. A well-known and even liked member of our staff has disappeared. His name—G. Wert. Never high in our confidence, he was yet a leading instructor in our Department of Foreign Enthusiasm, and an expert in Round Tableship and the Exchange of Unpleasantries. Last certainly seen at Ghent (office of our *L'Institution Vie-malheureuse*), glimpsed at Algiers, he probably passed, as a shadow, over the Peloponnesian border and disappeared behind the Iron Curtain. Wherever he is, he has taken his

secrets with him, and we now suffer the chagrin of listening, at Round Table conferences, to elementary Lifegambits from—why not name them?— the Russians. Thus has been inaugurated the era of Marxmanship in the conferences between East and West. Small wonder that the study of Lifemanship and Counter-lifemanship is regarded now as the still more urgent need of all of us.

Universityship.

L.C.C. (Lifemanship Correspondence College) is no substitute for three years' academic study at one of the older universities, and we have never made this claim. What we do intend, in our six-weeks' course, is that the student should learn how to be top student, and, when he is launched on the world, how to become the post-graduate top post.

To help us in our work here, university groups form spontaneously, send us their suggestions, or just write saying "How to help?"

When I get these letters from young Lifestudents, many of them little more than Lifeboys, from Professors, too, of all denominations, my answer to the question is always "Write about *yourself*, how *you* got away with it, how *you* think it is possible to get by the examiners without actually cheating. Express *yourself*."

FIG. 5. EDINBURGH, 1851.

While his friends are working late on the night before the examination, fellow-student distracts them by playing bagpipes outside their windows. Amazing that this example of primitive gamesmanship took place *in the year of the Great Exhibition*.

Why the Silence of Yale?

The response, entirely unsolicited, has been extraordinary. Oxford and Cambridge have helped with their maturer views; Edinburgh, Bangor and Leeds, in that order, have been perhaps more brilliantly experimental. Stanford, California, is at work, and Harvard has been especially forward with advice and publication. From Yale—I just want to record this as a simple statement—there has been no communication whatever.

The Harvard-Edinburgh.

It has been our function to sift and co-ordinate these contributions. To make it clearer to new readers, it can be said that we include in our studies the study of study, and fulfil our function as university University. It is the science of Scientific Attitudeship which we teach; the art of Arts.

I head this section "The Harvard-Edinburgh" because it will serve to introduce a specifically *Universityship* study theme on which we like to prove our mettle—the basic approach, really, to the examination-room. How to be one up on the lay student before the examinations have started; or how (passmanship) to excel after it is all over. Edinburgh specialises in the former; Harvard in the latter.

The phrase "To edinburgh" implies a spreading, a dissemination of despondency among other students working for Lifeman's examination by an appearance of solid knowledge, of calmness in the face of approaching crisis, and of a desire to help. In his inaugural address, as Senior President to the Edinburgh University Lifemanship Research Group,[1] J. Weatherhead was particularly careful to stress the fact (to use his own words) that the Undergraduateman must give one of two impressions, either that (1) he does nothing but work, or (2) that he does not work. Concentrating on (1), he describes the work of J. Reid, who specialises in striding into the reading-room with his hat on, going "straight to the shelves of a subject he is not necessarily studying,"[2] taking a book out as if he knew where to look for it, running down a reference and walking out again *quietly but plonkingly*.

Over the faces of student watchers nervousness runs like a whisper; though in fact Reid has just picked up a book of quotations to verify a clue in a crossword puzzle. By an accumulation of such featherweight ploys as these,[3] Reid was able to oppress his fellow-students with a sense of the hopelessness of any effort of theirs in the face of such competition, and many a promising degree man is virtually failed before he has set foot in the examination-room.

"To harvard" is, conversely, to seem, even when the examination is only two days off, to be totally indifferent to the impending crisis, and be seen walking calmly and naturally about, out of doors,

[1] 29th January, 1951. [2] Wider Interests Play.
[3] I believe that after putting the book back Reid sometimes speaks quietly to a shy-looking girl student *seeming to impart information to her*, as if to help her.

enjoying the scenery and taking deep breaths of air.[1]

Naturally, many Edinburgh men also harvard, and vice versa. But to maintain the truly contemporary nature of their native gambit, Harvard has its own special team—most of them on the teaching staff—with whom I am kept in touch.[2] A recent formulation is that of J. Smail's. This is Smail's wording. ("FitzJames" is a fictitious name):

Famed Harvardman (as distinct from Harvard man) J. FitzJames disappeared suddenly from College midway through January Reading Period, just about the time his friends began studying in earnest. Then, on the day of his first exam, he would return, strolling into the examination-room five minutes late, dressed in a light Palm Beach suit and heavily tanned. Sitting down next to a friend he would inspect his papers casually, and begin to write slowly.

Later it becomes known that FitzJames has received an A in the course. What is the explanation? FitzJames has been holing himself up in a miserable rented room in Boston surrounded by the total reading assignment, including the optional books, and has been working like a dog for three weeks, stripped to the waist between two sun lamps.

A certain sum of money has been allocated at Harvard for the preparation of a counter to this gambit. Even if the results arrive too late to be printed in this volume, I believe that by concentrating on an aspect of *one* of our activities, Universityship, I have given readers some insight into the *whole*.

[1] *"Don't harvard"* I once, when a visitor to Worcester, Oxford, heard, during a pleasant outing with the Chameleon Club, shouted after an undergraduate who, walking to the bathroom on or about 18th June, was humming.
[2] See *Harvard Alumni Bulletin*, 9 Feb., 1952.

II

DOCTORSHIP

M.D.-MANSHIP, PATIENTSHIP
AND THE HEALTH PLOY

I BELIEVE THAT our College treatment of Medicine illustrates our aims and methods as well as any. Basic medical studentship, doctorship and patientship provide us with the three "Threes" of Lifemanship teaching. Medical studentship is perhaps too advanced for the lay reader, and we have reserved for a privately-printed edition a technical note on the work of Canada in this sphere.

Our ten-days' course for young doctors—how different, in its brevity, compression and point, from the seven *years* of grinding work in the more orthodox schools of medical education. Not that this latter must be neglected, but we do claim that in our Demonstrator in Harleyship and our Sir J. Boot Reader we have two extraordinarily fine men who can give a helping hand both during and after the period of academic study, not only in the simple Health ploys but also in the establishment of one-up relations between doctor and doctor and doctor and patient and vice versa.

Health and the Normal Lifeplay.

Ordinary *health*, remember, is highly gambit-prone. Novice Lifemen are often seen sparring with each other in the friendly cut-and-thrust of the Health move.

"It's only a scratch" is often the first Life-remark of the prattling Lifechild, and the reply made by the infant only slightly less young ("Well, that is a good fing, anyhow") is often the first counter.

In later life it is soon discovered that a slight disability, properly used, can be advantageous, particularly where a desire to live up to a reputation for genius is required. We demonstrate the imperious stammer, the attention-inviting tremor and the romantic limp.[1]

Köhler was our first lecturer in this subject, and opposite our portrait of Byron you will see a diagram of the human figure crossed by a wavy line, known as "Köhler's Line." Köhler, originally a systematic botanist, attempted to standardise what he called "O.K. complaints" for various walks of life, above the line being in general more O.K. than below the line, though this varied interestingly, as can be imagined, in the case of such contrasted pursuits as those of poet, plasterer, racing driver and diplomat, to name a few.

---

[1] In the lecture-room, where we teach limpmanship and the use of the silver-headed cane, there is a large oil-painting of Byron to remind us that the present decay of Sir Walter Scott's reputation is in no small measure due to the fact that although Scott's limp was just as bad and just as genuine as Byron's, nobody ever heard about it. The Walter Scott picture was removed from the walls.

Odoreida-ism was rife in the early days of health-manship—with Odoreida's irritating "You're looking remarkably fit" to Gattling just after he'd been thrown over by Claudia; or his "You're looking a bit cheap" to Cogg just after Cogg had been attempting to brown himself for ten dangerous days in the Engadine. In general, I believe we have inculcated in our young Lifemen the rule that one must be able clearly to suggest either that one is absolutely healthy or, alternatively, never really free from pain. The two styles MUST NOT BE MUDDLED. On this basis all good health work must be grounded.[1]

Natural One-upness of Doctors.

But the first real hurdle to be tackled by the novice Healthman, when he comes of age, is the Doctor. We Lifemen have always been well-disposed towards doctors. Above all professions, except perhaps that of the expert in commercial law, the Box Office Manager, and the man whose special job it is to advise people about having their cars decarbonised, doctors have shown themselves to be apt and natural Lifemen, and their careers are built on a well-sprung framework of ploys and gambiting.

As some readers will not know, there is a *Lancet*[2] Research Group, denominating and codifying procedures. They have defined "Doctorship," with a

---

[1] An effective statement in the right context can sometimes be: "I have had 140 days' illness in my life." Listeners are unable, without a lame pause for calculation, to know whether to commiserate or admire.

[2] The official organ of British Medicine, and recognised by us.

rough directness, as "the art of getting one up on the patient without actually killing him."[1] Yes, but doctors, it must be remembered, are subjected to the healthy rivalry of Lifemanship from the very beginning of their training; and almost as soon as they are qualified they must decide (see *Lancet* Research) on whether to become one of four basic Doctor types.

Type One is the Damn-good-doctor, on the spot, enthusiastic, breathing common sense, fond of simple remedies, and opposed to *Type Two*, the Damn-good-scientist. Damn-good-scientist prides himself on having "forgotten the starting symptoms of chicken-pox." He "hasn't listened to a chest since his Finals year." His clothes are stained with chemicals. The bulge in his pocket is graph-paper, not a stethoscope.[2]

A rarer but effective type is (*Three*) the man, continuously being caught out of reach of normal hospital equipment,[3] who learnt his Infectious Diseases in the stagnant marshes of the Naquipl foothills, where he was the only doctor in 15,000 square miles, if that. Finally there is (*Four*) the doctor who achieves eminence by always replying to the simplest possible question (after the smallest conceivable pause): "Alas, we don't know."

[1] "Nursemanship," the art of getting one up on the doctor and/or the patient without actually marrying either, is also described, with subsidiary anti-Sister ploys and contra-Matron gambits.

[2] Additional *Lancet*-sponsored properties include a corked test-tube of soapy water in the waistcoat pocket, a tuft of guinea-pig fur on the lapel, and the use of odd bits of cardiac catheter, instead of string, to tie things up with.

[3] "St. Kildaship." This nineteenth-century term is no longer in use.

These types, potentially one up as each of them is, can be perpetually at war in the age-old struggle for the Survival of the Lifest. It is always the doctor who knows best how to appear to possess a better car than his nearest rival. The doctor who knows how to be one up in consulting-room equipment and clothes. (For our suggested diagonalising of clothes in relation to mean fashionable address, the top hat in the outer suburbs and the old fishing jacket for Harley Street, with gradations between, *see* Illustration below.)

Natural One-downness of Patient.

What chance, it may well be asked, has even the lay lifeman against the doctor? The doctor holds all the cards, and can choose his own way of playing them. Right at the start, when answering Patient's

FIG. 6. DOCTORSHIP: CROFT'S LAW OF INVERSE SUPERFICIAL DIFFERENTIATION IN TERMS OF MEAN EVOLUTIONARY ADDRESS. Correct clothes for (1) 6A Verlaine Road, Portsea, Hants.; (2) "Fordingbridge," Dunting Road, Basingstoke; (3) 16 Redcliffe Gardens, Kensington; (4) 14 Wimpole Street, W.1; (5) President of the Royal College of Physicians.

original telephone call, for instance, he can, and generally does, say "Dr. Meadows speaking" in a frightfully hollow and echoing voice, as if he was expecting a summons to sign a death certificate. Alternatively, a paralysingly brisk voice can be used suggesting that Doctor is busier than Patient in normal life, and in a more important way.

DOCTOR: Hallo, yes. Finchingfield here. . . . Well, it will have to be rather late this morning, I'll see what I can do.

In the bedroom, this brisk type of M.D.-man is tidier, better or at any rate more crisply dressed than the Patient, and is able to suggest by his manner not only that Patient's room is surprisingly disordered, but that he, the Doctor, goes in for a more up-to-date type of pyjamas than the ones he observes Patient to be wearing.

The Patient starts perkily enough. . . .

LAYMAN: Thank you, Doctor. I was coming home rather late last night from the House of Commons——

M.D.-MAN: Thank you . . . now if you'll just let me put these . . . hair brushes and things off the bed for you . . . that's right . . .

LAYMAN: I was coming home rather late. Army Act, really——

M.D.-MAN: Now just undo the top button of your shirt or whatever it is you're wearing . . .

LAYMAN: I say I was coming——

M.D.-MAN: Now if you've got some hot water—really hot—and a clean towel.

LAYMAN: Yes, just outside. The Postmaster-General . . .

M.D.-MAN: Open your mouth, please.

To increase the one-downness, bring in the washing-the-hands gambit immediately after touching hands with Patient. Unpleasant infectant possibilities can be suggested.

The old, now discarded, bedside mannership is still used when Doctor wishes to subdue the sensitive Patient suffering from an eclipsing headache. Doctor used to begin a constant fire of hollowly exploding clubroom stories, so involved in their climax that only the keenest attention revealed the point of expected laughter. We now teach that M.D.-man should show an *inaccurate familiarity with the Patient's own tastes or profession.* He can suggest, for instance, that some prized first edition "might be worth something some day," or, if his patient is a horseman, tell him that the first syllable in "Pytchley" is long. For actor-patients Doctor can tell the story of how as a young student he dressed up as Principal Boy in the Middlesex Hospital Pantomime when a member of the Middlesex Mauve Merriments.

After this opening treatment, Doctor may *under certain circumstances* ask Patient his symptoms. But he will let it be seen that he is not listening to what Patient is saying, and may place his hand on Patient's wrist, or, better, stomach, as if to suggest that he as Doctor can tell more through the sensitive tip of one finger than from listening to the layman's self-deceiving, ill-observed and hysterically redundant *impressions* of what is wrong with him.

Many good M.D.-men make a point of shepherding

their patients into the consulting-room where, by his way of averting his head as Patient is undressing, Doctor can suggest criticism of his choice of under-clothes, socks, &c. The doctor is well; patient is ill: and (if only because he is longing for a cigarette) in more ways than in mere physical health.

Nevertheless the following *Friendly* Consulting-room Approach[1] is basically better. Suppose your patient comes in with, say, a chronic outbreak of warts on the back of the neck. He will be disposed to make light of this. ALLOW HIM TO, BUT FRIGHT-EN HIM AT THE SAME TIME, by little asides to invisible nurses. Thus.

M.D.-MAN: Well, you are a pretty sight. Now, just lower your shirt.

LAYMAN (*enjoying himself*): Not very pretty for sun-bathing at Annecy next summer. I thought——

M.D.-MAN: Better take it right off. Ah, you lucky man. You know the lake, do you? (*Lowering voice*) Nurse, get me a Watson-Dunn, will you?

LAYMAN: Yes, I love it, we go every year . . .

M.D.-MAN (*pressing buzzer*): The food of course is mar-vellous. (*Speaking calmly into some machine*) Oh, Barker, get me the light syringe from the steriliser—yes, the dual. Yes, we must get you right for that.

LAYMAN: But it's not anything——

M.D.-MAN: Nothing serious, I'm sure. Now bend down. Yes, Annecy—and you know Talloires? . . . Now nurse, if you'll just stand by while we have a look.

[1] This gambit was invented by a well-known actor, with medical tastes. Shunning publicity, he yet allows me to say that it was evolved in Rome during the filming of *Quo Vadis*. He was in charge of the St. John's Ambulance Tent, Block L, during the scenes when the lions were eating the Christians—largely faked. He himself was playing the part of the Emperor Ustinian.

Quadriceps, please . . . and—oh, thank you, Barker. Better get the hydrogeniser going (*compressed air sound can be imitated by some assistant in the background going "zzzz" through his teeth*). Yes, there's a little restaurant—right down, please—the Georges Bise . . . Now.

At the end, with a charming "au revoir," M.D.-man, instead of telling him what is wrong, can stare, last thing, at frightened Patient's left eye through a specially contrived speculum which startles Patient with a view of Doctor's own eye, enlarged, inverted and bloodshot (*see* Illustration below).

Some Slight Discomfortship.

Doctorship Basic is, of course, to suggest that Patient is worrying either (*a*) too little, but (*b*) far more generally, too much. If (*a*), a good general suggestion is that he is playing games too violent for his time of life. "No ping-pong after 26," he will say. Or: "After 55, more than 18 holes is . . . well . . ." But for the more

FIG. 7. DR. J. HOLLIS CARTER'S EEZISLIPON.

This "speculum" is fitted with coated lenses which flash in the eye of the perturbed patient a magnified portion of doctor's face upside down.

"Sign manual of the well-run clinic."—*Scotsman.*

"Induces Cheyne-Stokes respiration and a Watts-Dunton anxiety."
—*Lancet.*

common "Don't make such a fuss" approach, procedure usually recommended for M.D.-men is as follows:

1. If Patient has a rash, describe some really serious skin disease seen in hospital that morning, as if this mentioning of a few silly spots was futile.

2. For stiff neck, put on an obviously assumed interest, say: "I'm sorry to hear of that," and if Patient says he has been woken up six times during the night by really sharp twinges, be overheard saying to some assistant that: "Patient appears to have had some slight discomfort. I shall not be in to lunch to-day."

3. When treating a cold, Doctor can go rather mechanically through a list of prescriptions, remedies and a routine which the patient "must" follow and then say: "I've got just the same sort of cold myself, they're about everywhere. What do *I* do about it? Well, personally I do nothing whatever. Absolutely nothing, I'm sorry to say. Just go on as if nothing had happened. What? Bed, that is my orders to you." All the time, Doctor is suggesting that his constitution, character, inherited resistance, courage and will-power are in every way stronger than Patient's.

Gambit Four is for Patient who wants to be made a fuss of. His warts are painful. His neck is swollen. Make him feel a fool by writing down everything he says. Thus:

M.D.-MAN: When did you first notice all this?
LAYMAN: My neck began to get a bit red . . . end of last month.

M.D.-MAN (*writing*): "End of month . . . neck becomes red . . ."

LAYMAN: They didn't really hurt till last week.

M.D.-MAN: "After eighteen days . . . some discomfort." Yes. This is the eighth case of false warts I've seen this week.

LAYMAN: What do you mean, false?

M.D.-MAN: Only the root is involved.

Modern Methodship.

Many Doctors, of course, use Modern Methodship, which consists in irritating or upsetting the patient by the totally irrelevant diagnostic approach. E.g. In comes the man with warts. M.D.-man takes one glance at the warts and then asks him to lie down.

M.D.-MAN: Right. Relax. Now when did you first notice the warts?

LAYMAN: Oh, about . . . months ago.

M.D.-MAN Right. Now try lifting the right leg slowly . . . down . . . now turn the foot sharply to the left—no, *left.* Now sit up. Up. Do you ever relax?

LAYMAN: Oh—*yes.*

M.D.-MAN: No—I mean every muscle, cheeks, nose, gums . . .

FIG. 8. M.D.-MANSHIP.

A simple method of making patient feel a fool. If he complains of ear-ache after bathing, examine his plantar surfaces.

The Totally Irrelevant Question can be brought in here. This is sometimes known as Allergyship.

M.D.-MAN: Tell me, what sort of nail varnish does your wife use?

LAYMAN (*beginning to get sour*): Not married.

M.D.-MAN: Not? Do you keep chickens under your bedroom window?

LAYMAN: Sloane Avenue Mansions doesn't encourage chickens.

M.D.-MAN: Of course not. Look, now, do you mind if I have a look at your fountain-pen? Yes. Thanks. (*Pause*). Yes.

Opposed to this is

Traditional Methodship.

Traditional Methodship consists in blurting out every now and then something about "what she wants isn't psycho-howsit or even deep-ray thingummy but a good slap on the whatsisname." If Patient turns out to be really ill after all, it is always possible to look grave and proud at the same time, and say, "You realise, I suppose, that twenty-five years ago you'd have been dead?"[1]

[1] We are working at the moment on a new and somewhat contrasted technique of alarming patients, which we call the Factor of Uncertain Trust. In its present rough state we keep it to a footnote. The doctor adopts a man-to-man attitude, and admits right away that he is not quite sure. To give the wording advised by our visiting Welbeck Demonstrator, C. Hobbs:

M.D.-MAN: Let's have a look at these warts. (*Begins to whistle a slow tune*) They *are* warts, are they? But isn't there something that looks rather like a wart which you have to take out, or something? Wait a minute—where's my book? Where's Price—big red—here it is. Funny, they haven't got anything about warts in the index. Some long-winded medical word, I suppose . . . here's something. Oh, yes, it says: "Inject with novo-phosthene." Do you mind if I

The Need for Organised Patientship.

It will be seen that the whole doctor-patient situation bristles with difficulties for the layman. But is it not precisely this kind of problem—this apparently fixed one-upness of doctors—which we of L.C.C. like best to tackle?

In homely language, how can the Patient get back?

Divers approaches to the problem were attempted in the early days, only to be discarded. It used to be thought that it would curb the Doctor's high spirits to be asked if, after diagnosing mumps, he "would mind bringing in another opinion." But it was soon discovered that the doctor's solemn expression concealed a delight in being able to get an extra fee for poor old Pettinglass.

Some success is reported from married couples who have trained their youngest child to say in a clear voice, "Mummy, I don't like that man" whenever a doctor comes into the room. This is now not much used.

---

just look that up? Little grey book somewhere. No, I haven't got novo-phosthene, but I've got something damned like it. Damned like it. Now, we're supposed to use a squeegee. Oh Lord, I haven't used one of those things for years. Supposed to put it under the tap. All these "do's" and "don'ts." Now then. . . . Now look, you're going to help me. If you'd just mind pushing . . . (*begins a jolly laugh*) Go on, push against it! Push!

A refinement of this gambit has just been received from Ireland. If Price is missing from the Doctor's shelf, as it probably will be, let him take down a book titled in large letters *Veterinary Surgery*. Or, better still, (S. Casey suggests) *A Simple Manual for Dog Lovers*.

Marvellous Little Manship.

This is a proved doctor-irritant, especially if the ploy is executed by a well-dressed woman patient visiting Harley Street address of physician holding dignified position at London Hospital—one who prides himself particularly on never being guilty of Harleyship *per se*.

Recommended dialogue runs as follows:

LIFEWOMAN: I was wondering whether that marvellous little man in Curzon Street would be able to help me, Doctor?

HARLEYMAN: Oh yes? What little man?

LIFEWOMAN: Olaf Pepacanek. *How* do you pronounce it?

HARLEYMAN: I'm afraid I've never heard of him.

LIFEWOMAN: Oh, but he's a most marvellous man— he *weighs* everything. He says that English doctors don't realise that what he calls the square foods and the round foods can cancel each other out. He's written a book.

HARLEYMAN: Oh yes.

LIFEWOMAN: It's called *Bricks Without Straw*.

HARLEYMAN: Oh yes.

This is often quite irritating. Our Wimpole Reader, Gattling-Fenn, is working on what he calls rather long-windedly the Patient's Deskside Manner Counter to the Doctor's Bedside Approach. In the consulting-room, the doctor is tapping Gattling's chest. Gattling exudes a confident cheerfulness.

DOCTOR: (*Taps*).

GATTLING: Tap away.

DOCTOR: Now the back.

GATTLING: Thorough is as thorough does. You chaps certainly put us through the hoop nowadays.

DOCTOR: Say ninety-nine.

GATTLING: Dial 999, yes? (*Sings*) I'm ninety-nine to-day, I'm ninety-nine to-day.

DOCTOR: Keep still, please.

GATTLING: Still as a mouse.

DOCTOR: Quiet.

GATTLING (*Pause, begins to laugh*): I suppose it's all necessary, but my great-uncle was a bit of a sawbones. Doctors were doctors in those days. Anyhow, I know *he* was able to take his old wooden stethoscope and diagnose lobar pneumonia through two woollen vests and a horse-hair overcoat in thirty seconds dead.[1]

Under examination, Gattling would counter the danger of nudeship ("the natural one-downness of the unclothed"[2]) by arranging telephone calls direct to the consulting-room carefully timed to coincide with the maximum unclothed condition. He had himself rung by an aristocratically confident female voice and would then become involved in a long conversation, obviously with some wealthy and attractive girl, and burst out twice into long telephone laughter, slapping his bare thigh and shouting: "This is colossal! Tell me more!" (Bell.)

Further minor counter-doctor ploys are:

G.M.C.-manship, defined as the "playing on the doctor's fears of seeming to seek either publicity or kudos for medical qualifications which in fact he does not possess."

---

[1] *Lancet*-sponsored phrasing.
[2] Many will recognise this as the phrase inscribed under the dome of the Hunterian amphitheatre at St. George's Hospital.

It is possible to throw doubt on the very term doctor—"I am, I suppose, right in calling you 'Doctor'?" Again, if the doctor asks, "Don't you think your symptoms have a psychological basis?" (always a weak ploy), reply at once, "I had no idea that was one of your subjects. I have always wanted a good psycho-therapist." Refuse to take in his worried assurance that he is not a trained psychiatrist. You "will tell your friends" about him.

Under this same heading, if Doctor tells Patient that he has been spending the week-end in deepest Bucks where he saw, say, Bob Hope and his niece, Patient can reply : "Hope told me, and—surprise for you!—that snap Babette took of you and Bob joking together with a stethoscope in the bathing-pool is being published in the *Tatler*."

In contrast with this there is:

Title Play, which consists in annoying your personal consultant by pretending to think that all doctors like titled patients. Talk in what is called the Titles Voice about your friend Max Bodenheim who has just been flown over to Dublin to have a look at the Connemaras' little girl and her tiresome attack of thrush. Even if this does not irritate your doctor it will certainly get him off beat. Some Lifemen add: "I must see if I can get you one or two little plums like that."

Certain patients, especially at Christmas-time or on other festive occasions, go to extraordinary lengths to make the doctor feel awkward after a consulting-room examination. When re-dressing, for

41

instance, they will roll their collar-stud under the doctor's couch, grope for it, and appear to "find" either a small medicine bottle half-full of crème de menthe, or a set of false teeth embedded in a meringue.[1] It only remains to ask: "Are these yours?" in a plonking tone of voice, and the usual results follow.

Specialist Counter-Lifepatient Play.

An intensely effective ploy often used by M.D.-men but overlooked in their published researches is for Doctor to treat Patient not only as if he knew nothing about medicine but as if Patient were as ignorant of all anatomical knowledge as a child of four. Often M.D.-men will give totally unnecessary technical names and then explain them—e.g. "that mild rhinitis of yours: sniffles to you." However determined the Lifepatient may be to show his knowledge, the trained M.D.-man will get him down in the end. Using the Warts background again, the dialogue might go like this:

LIFEPATIENT (*knowledging*): I came to you because trivial as the condition looks there was this distinct œdematous area under the warts.

M.D.-MAN: Yes, it is a bit puffy. Tell me, does it go *Pong*-pong, *Pong*-pong?

LIFEPATIENT: You mean does it throb? Are the growths vascular?

M.D.-MAN: Now don't you worry about that. You see, the heart is a sort of pump——

LIFEPATIENT: Yes—please—but . . .

M.D.-MAN: It goes squeez-o, squeez-o—no, look at my hand.

[1] Both supplied by Lifemanship Accessories, Ltd.

42

LIFEPATIENT: I am, but——

M.D.-MAN: And the blood isn't just blood, it's full of little soldiers, all fighting against each other.

LIFEPATIENT: Yes.

M.D.-MAN: Have you ever been in the army?

LIFEPATIENT: Well, no, but——

M.D.-MAN: You've heard the word "corpuscles." Those are the white fellows and the red chaps. Now this is how the battle begins. At the source of the infection— where Something's Wrong——

Even experienced Lifepatients can be silenced in the end by this treatment. Easier to deal with is the Harleyman who tries to put you in your place when you go to him for a stiff neck by suggesting that you are being rather trivial and he is feeling rather tired, "up all night transfusing a couple of touch-and-go cases of thrombocytopenic purpura."

It is always possible for Lifepatient to reply: "I'm sorry to have bothered you with this apparently trivial thing, but my friend Eddie Webb-Johnson[1] persuaded me to go to a really competent general physician if I could find one. He prodded me about for twenty minutes or so and told me to let him know the results of a more careful examination; and who was doing it, what were his qualifications, and so on.

"By the way—just to stop him bothering—what are your qualifications?"

Cust's Ploy of Poise.

There is no doubt that the best of all counter-doctor techniques is some application of the vast

[1] Or some equally absolutely O.K. medical name.

Poise Gambit which we are elaborating now for inclusion in Volume IV. Perfected by Miss Antigone Cust, it consists in the overcoming of any crisis by the fixing of the profile in one of six recommended positions and the maintaining, however urgent the cue for a reply, of almost complete silence.[1] The sole word which Miss Cust allows herself to utter is some admonition, spoken in a slightly American intonation, to "relax."

The only answer to this gambit so far evolved by our countership department and recommended for doctors is to say either (*a*) "I haven't relaxed for sixteen years" or (*b*) "What are you poised *for*?"

Fig. 9. Hunter-Dawson's "Tri-try."
(For taking second opinion.)

---

[1] Beginners in "profiling," as it is called, are reminded that Miss Cust owes her success to the possession of perfect classical features. The gambit should not be attempted by others whose noses are (*a*) button- or (*b*) blob-shaped.

III

BUSINESSMANSHIP

1. The Problem

YEOVIL'S SCHOOL OF Businessmanship is not yet
fully formed. It is a strange fact, which we here state
in all frankness and without criticism, that vast as
are its resources, the business world has made small
contribution to our funds. "We invented Lifemanship before you were born," said a bulk-buyer of
synthetic soup by-products to me the other day, and
this conveys the attitude of the whole business community. "Certainly," said his friend, who disposed
of the residue of the soup by-products, which he
patented as compressed fuel. "And didn't we invent
the word Salesmanship?"

"Yes, and Chairmanship too," said a heavy-
jowled older man, who bought up the remains of the
residue of this soup by-product for his firm "Natural
Broths, Ltd."

And of course one must sympathise with this view.
"Businessmanship = Salesmanship = Lifemanship"
... and yet. At any rate, when the concrete request
came for guidance, a request from the business
quarter of New York City, we were glad to add this
youngest of all our student courses to our schedule.

Lifemanship's Principle of Negative Selling.

What is our approach? On the wall of Commercial Corner, in the East Wing of our College, there hangs a picture. It is taken from the wrapper of a popular American Salesmanship Manual.[1]

FIG. 10. THE "ALL-PURPOSE PICTUREGRAM". (*See text.*)

("It's men like you we want."
Alternatively
"It's men like me you want.")

Look at the picture. On the left is a figure full of the confidence of the man who knows his job and knows it is well done. The Salesman. On the right is the prospective client, the "Prospect," his eagerness to buy only matched by his astonished admiration of this fine and courageous personality who is hypnotising him into a deal which his reason abhors. That is the implied interpretation.

There you have the business of Business. But in Businessmanship the roles must be reversed. The sitting figure on the *right* is the salesman, trained by us in that bungling diffidence which alone can infuse confidence into the buyer and fill him with certainty that this feeble sap before him couldn't get the better of a milk pudding.

[1] This is the only picture in our Business lecture-room, because it can be used to illustrate the right and wrong methods of Salesmanship and anything else as well. E.g. I am sometimes asked, Is there a Lifeman's put-off for insurance salesman? Yes, there is, and this

The No-Pen Approach.

For our first simple lesson we demonstrate the basic gambit of the No-Pen Approach—easy phrase to remember. Childishly primary, it yet embodies Lifemanship's Principle of Negative Selling.

Lay businessmen when they are anxious—typical business incident—to persuade a client to sign some document containing a clause which on closer inspection will be seen to be to the client's disadvantage, sometimes do it like this. With the document on the desk, the dialogue follows some such Wrong Course as this:

Lay BUSINESSMAN: I think you'll find everything quite in order, Mr. Fortinbras.

FORTINBRAS: Oh yes, but what about the——

L.B. (*oiling in*): You did want us to keep mutually independent? Now, you sit here.

FORTINBRAS (*puzzled*): Something about "giving you right of transference"?

L.B.: That's right.

FORTINBRAS (*suspicious*): Yes, but——

L.B.: Now, if you just put your name where I pencilled it in. I think you'll find my pen in working order . . .

---

picture demonstrates it. In Method One, the "prospect" (left) is countering the insurance salesman (right) by a sudden stream of praise for insurance policies in general and a suggestion, since the salesman earns his living by talking, that *he* should insure either (*a*) his hard palate or (*b*) his right fist, essential in forceful speech and especially liable to accident. In Method Two, Prospect (right) is asking salesman (left) if he would mind continuing the conversation at home, take pot-luck with his aunts, and give a comic recitation to help entertain the displaced children of the Papercutters' Orphanage—"they're quite all right if you know how to handle them, and we ought to be back before 1 a.m."

What is wrong? The untrained businessman is standing ready with a gleaming fountain-pen full of rich ink. He is hovering. He is amiable. Client is put on the defensive, and ten to one he will begin to ask questions.

Contrast now the *Lifemanship-trained* Businessman in the same position. Once more the document is on the table, all ready for Mr. Fortinbras.

BUSINESS LIFEMAN: I think this is the thing you're supposed to sign.

MR. FORTINBRAS: I beg your pardon?

B.L.: Only for goodness' sake let's make sure. Must get my secretary to tidy my desk.

F. (*amused*): Well, here's my name, anyhow.

B.L.: Let's try and take it in. (*Reading very slowly*) "Whereas the party hereinafter called the copyholders shall within the discretion of both signatories"—can't understand a word.

F. (*almost paternal already*): Let me. I'm used to this sort of jargon. "The parties assigned . . ."

B.L.: Look. Wonderful, isn't it? (*They laugh.*)

F. (*taking charge*): That's right, and I'm supposed to sign these—paragraphs individually, aren't I?

B.L.: Oh? I mean *yes*. Awfully sorry, don't seem to have a pen (*rustles through papers*). I'm most awfully sorry, I've got a new secretary. Josephine! Probably at coffee. Typical.

F.: It's all right, I've got a pen.

B.L. (*keen for the first time*:): Oh, isn't that the new sort that writes on ice, or something? Marvellous little thing. Can I look at it? Sorry, after you.

"Sorry," because client is already in the act of signing the document. The client is helping. To make assurance doubly sure in this technique, it is

no bad thing if businessman actually puts client's
borrowed pen into his own pocket, after admiring it,
as if by mistake. Client now leaves, not only having
signed the paper but full of a queer sort of confidence.
This signature technique was first perfected by
Lumer Farr, and it is known as Lumer's Bumbling
Approach.[1]

This negative fountainpenmanship sets the note of
our course. We teach students to remember that it
is only men *below* the highest quality in any firm who
take exact measurements of the carpet in their office
room to make sure it is not narrower than Y's or less
thick than Z's. But in Supreme Boss-ship we always
teach plainness, simplicity and downright ordinari-
ness. No Yeovil-trained managing director ever
dreams of being seen behind a desk clanking with
telephones, loudspeakers, soft speakers, buzzers, little
flashing lights, and silver boxes overflowing with
splendid cigarettes and engraved with the signatures
of supposedly affectionate colleagues. No. Take
Lumer Farr, Yeovil-trained Vice-president (life-
word for Complete Boss) of International Packing
Cases. "You'd never think," I have heard people

[1] In Missouri a fine parallel ploy is in use, invented by St. Louis's
First Lifeman, G. Palen—"St. Louis One," to give him his proper
title. To execute the ploy, used in first business contacts, the Life-
salesman "should be meticulously dressed, perhaps in a Homburg."
And then present not a shiny clean business card but *one which has
been torn, stained with coffee, apparently dipped in beer, sticky on the back, and
almost torn in half.* After giving card, Missouri asks for it back "*as it
is my only one.*" This lulling tactic is said to soften the hardest business heart, and when he was younger G. Palen, then first using his
broken card, is said to have received many offers of *free financial help*
from real-estate executives and leading industrialists, including
many in chemical research.

FIG. 11. MANAGING DIRECTOR'S DESK.
(a) Wrong.

say, "that Lumer Farr controlled three-quarters of the crude teak export trade of Canada." Actually he didn't, *but why should anyone think he did?*

Lumer likes to be called "The Guv'nor," but likes it to be thought that he likes to be called "Bert."[1] He creeps about in a little black coat. His desk is a plain deal table with nothing on it whatever. The only telephone in the room is an old-fashioned candlestick one in the corner with a winder. He gets up and answers it himself about twice during the morning. Guarding his room, of course, there are

[1] In the science of Christian-naming, Lumer is associated with Farr's Law of Mean Familiarity. This can be expressed by a curve, but is much clearer set down as follows:

The Guv'nor addresses

Co-director Michael Yates as	MIKE
Assistant director Michael Yates as . . .	MICHAEL
Sectional manager Michael Yates as . . .	MR. YATES
Sectional assistant Michael Yates as . . .	YATES
Indispensable secretary Michael Yates as . .	MR. YATES
Apprentice Michael Yates as	MICHAEL
Night-watchman Michael Yates as . . .	MIKE

FIG. 12.   MANAGING DIRECTOR'S DESK.
(*b*) Right.

ranks and ranks of fashionable men and women dressed as secretaries, whose function it is to be extremely busy and to keep anybody except some n'er-do-well nephew[1] from ringing up or speaking to Lumer. These rebuffs in which he has trained this group are delightfully contrasted with Lumer's occasional bemused and affable appearances at the doorway of his office, when he may ask you himself to come in, and apologises for the lack of courtesy with which you have been treated. Then he will fumble out a broken packet and offer you a twisted cigarette.

Lumer is always slipping out of the room and slipping into the room in a way which is supposed to be unnoticed, but which in fact everybody is supposed

[1] Lumer's "Ploy of the Ridiculously Soft Heart."   He always says, "Suppose I'd better speak to the young scallywag."   But he has never actually given him either help or money.

to notice. When he gets out of a car or a plane, or even coming out of the theatre, he will slip quietly away, head down, as if he were avoiding a reporter. And quite late at night he will be seen, by arrangement, alone at this empty desk, on the plain deal chair.

2. COMMITTEESHIP

I have enunciated a general principle: let me now outline the work of one of our study circles, Committeeship.

It is axiomatic that Committeeship is the art of coming into a discussion without actually understanding a word of what anybody is talking about. But this entry can only be made effective if the speaker *decides what sort of person he, the speaker, is, and sticks to it.* The sort doesn't much matter, consistency is what counts; but the following committeeship types are especially recommended:

Type One, MULSIPRAT. The man who, pretty high and perhaps chairman, is yet rather muddled. At the same time he is never in a flap about his mistakes, but says, "There I go again" or "There's another of my beauts."[1] This is endearing and in fact the point of Mulsiprat is being adored by everybody. He may employ two special secretaries, one male and one female, whose exclusive difficult duty is to[2] obviously adore him.

[1] May I gratefully acknowledge that the wording here, and certain other ploys in this section, were hacked out in committee with a dissatisfied group of low-ranking members of the editorial staff of *Fortune*.

[2] For our lifesponsored split infinitive, see our next publication, *Womanship*, 1954.

Type Two, GALEAD, is also rather mad. But this rather-madmanship is of a totally different sort. Galead is manic, never cuts nails, has one shoe-lace undone, wears new jackets *with one button missing*, reveals faint tremor of the left hand, chain-smokes (dummy nicotine stains may be varnished on to the backs of the fingers). He sometimes adds to this a speech-disability-sign—e.g. starting every remark with a long downward-cadence whistle—it (*whistle*) "cures my stammer."

In committee he is the permanently "difficult" one: "(*Whistle*) Yes, but *how*?" Early in the meeting he finds himself in definite disagreement with the Chairman and Managing Director on some minor issue, which makes it all the easier for him to be overwhelmingly on their side round about lunch-time.

FIG. 13. DIAGRAM OF MAN IN THE STREET.

Type Three, LUDLOW, is the tremendously ordinary chap, valuable because he is in close touch with tremendously ordinary people and can, himself, talk tremendously ordinarily.[1] We can't do without Ludlow, because he is the man in the street.

[1] Not to be confused with the man who talks tremendously ordinarily to children. See *Lifemanship* ("Week-endmanship").

FIG. 14. DIA-
GRAM OF MAN
NOT IN THE
STREET.
(Reduced
scale.)

Type Four, MAIDENHAIR, we draw especial attention to because he represents a totally new type, of high value, as we believe, and something we are perhaps rather specially proud of, because he has been developed entirely through Lifemanship-sponsored organisations. He is the man not in the street. Sometimes he has taken a First or possibly read a biography of Verdi.

Type Five, TEMPESTRIAN, is not brilliant at all but sensible. He counters suggestions of brilliant-type Maidenhair by saying "Yes, but don't let's forget the big picture. What, after all, are we trying to sell?"

Type Six, CO-AX, is in a way wicked, or at any rate puts business first and says so. In the world of journalism he is so hard-boiled about tender feelings that rival committeemen are thought to feel awe. His voice is thin and waxy. "What we want on this page here," he says, "is a picture of a displaced crippled sick orphan of exiled alien parents and plug it for all we're worth." One day we were discussing the insertion of a rather daring portrait of fairly pretty Paulette O. in our little mag. "Page Three," Co-ax said, hard-boiling. "We want sex on page three, nine inches by eight. Always assuming that we have a story about cruelty to animals on page seven." This always goes down particularly well with the shyer shareholders, who may be strong family men and churchwardens. "Co-ax knows his job," they say afterwards, downing their small gin-and-limes in one.

Type Seven, HOSPITER, can be any of the foregoing, and yet none. He is the natural counter-committeeman, the underminer. It is not what he is, but what he says, that matters.

Hospiter Parlettes, many of them silent, are as follows:

(*a*) When rival committeeman is speaking:
i. Look sadly at boots (it is best to have actual boots).
ii. Doodle and continue to doodle with the faintest possible deepening of the corners of the mouth. Try to suggest that you see something irresistibly inappropriate or comic in what your rival is saying, but wild horses wouldn't make you spoil his little speech by mentioning it now. This delicate and highly expert ploy was first described to me independently by H. Whyte and F. Anderson, and named by the latter the "Mona Lisa Ploy."

(*b*) When rival committeeman has finished speaking, say:
i. "Well, we sort of came to a decision about that, didn't we, after a fairly full discussion last week, a rather good discussion, I thought. I mean we agree."
Or alternatively say:
ii. "Well" (*pause and look hard at chairman, as if only you and he know this*), "there are definite reasons why that is going to become impracticable fairly shortly, aren't there?"
Or say:
iii. "Yes, but we have got to think of the effect on the ordinary nice people we meet in the street. They are not terribly brainy, but they are quite nice people really."

If rival makes obviously good bold and original point, counter it

(i) by saying: "Yes, I think that's a good idea—I wonder if we were right to discard it five years ago when there was all that row." Or

(ii) if you can only think of something conventional and commonplace as alternative, *make* your flat suggestion in an "of course I'm completely mad" voice (*Flairship*) and add: "I know you'll think I'm making a fool of myself, but I think some of us are bound to make fools of ourselves before anything really happens, don't you?" Or

(iii) simply say: "Yes, but that isn't really what we're discussing, is it?"

Regil and the Economics Ploy.

Type Eight, REGIL,[1] is different from all the foregoing if only because he knows, if possible, less about the subject under discussion, and the business of the committee generally, than anybody else present. He is rather like Maidenhair, the First in Classics, except that the general impression is that Regil took a First in Economics.

Regil invariably creates an economics wicket by referring everything to the social or monetary sciences. He often speaks of "structured behaviour" and uses the phrase "inner directed," frequently mixing it, according to Whyte of Manhattan, with a colloquialism ("He's pretty much of an inner-directed guy").

Regil, however, certainly comes into his best on his

[1] These titles may have some religious or cosmographical significance, or they may be the names of the first eight losers backed by us in the Yeovil Handicap, Spring 1952.

own subject, economics—"the plonking science," as Matthew Arnold called it; and it is generally agreed that almost any phrase from any chapter of this extraordinary subject will meet any emergency, if the sentences are spelt out sufficiently slowly and clearly.

Sometimes, of course, Regil, especially after a short snifter, enjoyed himself with a little wild incomprehensibility (*Economics Approach A*).

"If you want to influence the general liquidity situation of banks *and* public," he would say, pretending to expect a reply. "If you do," he would go on, "I think you're forgetting that the Bank of England's discretionary action on the cash basis took the shape of dealings in Treasury Bills, the market rate of discount on which could *and did* fluctuate."

Regil would firm up his voice a good deal on "did fluctuate." But he was always at his best, I thought, on the more classical *Economics Approach B* (the "Approach of Utter Obviousness").

This "stupefaction of the exhaustingly clear" (Watertower) was used by Regil at moments of some crisis. "I'm not going to tell you why most demand curves slope downwards," he would begin, as a paralyser. Then he would become clear, in that frightful way of his. "Unless something happens to change the state of demand," he said, as if he was quoting, and incredibly enough he was, "more will be bought at any given price than at any higher price."

Another pause, before the next sentence, when his voice became so cuttingly audible it seemed to pass straight to the centre of my head and short-cut the organs of comprehension completely: "Any rise in price WILL REDUCE THE VOLUME OF SALES."

Suddenly he was quiet again, for the homely instance:

"When a child enters a shop to buy a pennorth of bull's-eyes, *by the mere fact of asking for the bull's-eyes it incurs a debt of one penny*. Look——"

I knew this "look" of Regil's. It was the prelude to a sort of Economics Oration, which we were all too hypnotised to interrupt:

"Look, and what do you see?"
Generally I saw the ash-tray, steaming with unfinished cigarettes.
"You see the farm labourer in the fields, tending the cattle to be marketed. The factory workers controlling the machines, feeding them with raw materials which they *transform into manufactured produce*. The miner is extracting mineral deposits from the earth, the clerk is recording transactions in the office, transport workers are moving persons and goods from one place to another. By cable and wireless instructions are transmitted with amazing speed . . ."

And so it went on. The fact that most of us were always complaining of telephone delays, and that none of us had ever actually seen any of these things (except perhaps Rusper, the clerk), didn't stop Regil from having another of his recurrent successes, from flattening the committee into respectful silence, and from mounting, with one foot on "produce" and another on "goods," yet one more rung on Businessmanship's difficult ladder.

IV

CORRESPONDENCE COLLEGE

DEPARTMENT OF ART

THE COMPLETE PRINTED syllabus of our courses is available through the usual channels, but as the two schools I have so far described are both vocational, I am anxious to reassure readers that the Arts are not neglected at Yeovil. On the contrary, I doubt whether there is any department in which new ground is more obviously broken.

The Doing of the Doing.

Whereas most universities teach the history, function, practice and criticism of drama, music and the plastic arts, no attention whatever is given "to the doing of the doing"—i.e. to that natural one-upness which even the Lifeman visitor to theatre or concert can so unobtrusively suggest, and which the actual Life-artist, the creator, assumes as a natural right.   How often do we not find, in the pre-Games-lifemanship era, that the artist is actually one down?

De-Slading and Counter R.A.D.A.-ship.

Painters, writers and actors particularly find, to take one example, that our Corrective Course, for ex-students of the best establishments, is a blessing. "Opens a new world in a fortnight," wrote one.

Take a would-be writer who has just taken a First-class Honours in English Language and Literature at Oxford—Balliol, typically. What chance has he got of success in an author's career compared, say, to a tramp, a Lieutenant-General, or a photographer of East African animals?

Or take the R.A.D.A.-man—the dramatic student. He may have been trained and passed with Honours in basic movement, including basic sitting-down, a silver medallist in basic door-shutting, basic speech, basic silence and basic basic. But these accomplishments can scarcely be said to put him in the one-up position or make a Chapter Two for the theatrical autobiography which we generally recommend should be written at the age of twenty-four.

Humble Startship.

No. For genius-ship, a smooth beginning is fatal. In our Edmund Kean Wing we roughen these young actors, we put them through a course of Crummles-ship. In the constant smell of grease-paint, sprayed through special nozzles powered by diesel fans, we let them mingle with the dust of a typical green-room (painted by the Brothers Harker). They learn to juggle, to walk the tight-rope, to wander about in the flies, to go without food for thirty-six hours, while they wait to fetch pints of beer for a drunken stage-manager who teaches them nothing except

FIG. 15. THE COUNTER R.A.D.A. SCHOOL.

This drawing of the Potterphon, evolved for our Founder by F. Wilson for teaching students to act the mad scene in *Hamlet* under conditions of mean average distraction, is self-explanatory. Students will note (A) bell for simulating fire-engines passing down Shaftesbury Avenue; (B) tea-tray rattler; (C) paper-bag crumpler; (D) student-actress speaking the line "Here's rosemary, that's for remembrance"; (E) icy blast from wings; (F) dust from flies; (G) whiff of grease-paint; (H) whiff of beer; (J) tea attendants saying they haven't got change; (L) sweet-sucking; (M) orange-sucking, with whiff; (N) distant voice calling, "Star News Standard"; (O 1-5) coughs, whispers, etc., controlled by mixer; (P) the Founder; (Q-T) inattentive audition-holders.

how to receive an oath and a cuff.[1] We teach the
girls, while still in the dingy lodgings and unhealthy
surroundings which we provide, to step at one hour's
notice, still rubbing embrocation on bruises pitifully
redolent of stout, into some performance of, say,
Beatrice in *Much Ado* or Bridget in *While The.*[2] Between the acts they eat dummy steak and onions and
drink a pint of porter, then go home to the wretched
apartment of the travelling mummer. They may be
R.A.D.A.-women up to golden goblet standards, but
they will still be able to say, and feel, that once, in
the beginning, they were struggling in the hardest
school of all.

Counter-Slading.

A basically similar though outwardly totally different course is given to young art students who have
been Slading away for three years, admirably
taught, of course, Antique and Life, who have spent
the correct number of vacations in Paris and even
enjoyed the fruits of a Prix de Rome, thereby shut-
ting themselves off apparently irretrievably from
contact with the people, humble startship, naïve-
ship and spontaneous folk art.

Here again we supply the humble start and set
them to work locally, in the signal-box at the level-
crossing by the back of our garden, for instance,

---

[1] The post of this "stage-manager" is filled by Leonard Moppet of
Buttermere.
[2] We encourage professionally abbreviated names of the plays of
Shakespeare and Rattigan (*While the Sun Shines*). Actually, we shorten
them even more, sometimes calling *Much Ado*, *Much*.

where they have no time, labouring fourteen hours a day at the clerical duties of assistant-signalman, to think of easel and palette. Yet their art will begin to show itself in the decorations they will add, naïvely bold, painted on the gateposts of the level-crossing, or in chalk drawings of village wedding scenes rubbed on the back of the routine reports of changes in the railway time-table or dossiers of local goods trains. These we make a point of discovering after three months, whereupon, in little less than ten years, the the new artist has slightly more chance of placing his work in Bond Street, or at any rate of being noticed in Park Crescent.

V

A NOTE ON
EXHIBITIONSHIP[1]

The following paragraphs were issued at the request of the Arts Council on the occasion of the closing of the South Bank. We reprint them here unaltered.

"Exhibitionship" is the name for the various ploys and gambits connected with the art of being, or seeming to be, a visitor to an exhibition. It is not the art of exhibiting (Barryship).

The basic gambit is of course the achievement of the state of one-upness on the rest of the public. A word of advice, then, perhaps particularly to the foreigner—always welcomed to our country by the lifeman—on certain simple methods of visiting an exhibition.

Classical Wrong Approach.

Though there are confusing exceptions to this rule, British visitors to London go to exhibitions as a duty, not a pleasure. Note at the Zoo the fixed smile of the mother, determined to get through with it good-

[1] I am going to make no mention in this note of "Bonding," as it is miscalled, because this is dealt with in a special pamphlet Y.16, "Bonding for Beginners," which deals with what to say at the Redfern, what to say at the Lefevre and what to say at the Leicester, and other Bond Street Galleries not in Bond Street.

humouredly. Note, in the Egyptian Room of the British Museum, how grim the father and how quivering the elder sister. "Stand still, Frank," she says. Or, "You'll spoil everything," to an innocent child who is quietly fermenting, having been fed on nothing but starch since they all left Colchester by bus at six in the morning.

This is classical Wrong Approach. To be out of the ruck, be gay. Come into the Egyptian Room, if necessary, with a smile and a wink. Roar with laughter as you approach the neolithic flints. If with a young child, it is possible to increase this effect and sustain your reputation for child management at the same time by occasionally feeding it with the special glucose sweets we supply—dashed with opium or some other not quite harmless somniferent. "I think it's because we never say Don't," you say to a group of friends who are admiring the child's acquiescence. "She is rather sweet, isn't she?"

Practise on the Tate.

It is as well to practise all gambits on the permanent museums and exhibits before approaching any special collections or centenary shows.

Practise in the Tate Galley, for instance, not to shuffle grimly from picture to picture, not to hang one methodical minute before each exhibit. To achieve the one-up position, let it be known that you have "come to see the Steers." This refers of course to Steer the artist. Say that there is one particular Steer of a luminous seascape with a patch of elephant grey (do not say "a small battleship") on the horizon and if it is not on view it must be in the vaults and can you please have access to them.

It is a fairly good gambit, certainly at the Tate, to be friendly with the attendants. At any rate, address them by some name such as "Kemp," and say, "Good morning, Kemp. Is Mr. Laver in to-day?" "Mr. Laver" is what is called an "O.K. exhibition name." Or you can say, "Good afternoon, McIndoe, have you seen Sir Kenneth?"

With pictures, and with art in general, it is rather a good thing not to go to the places where everybody else goes. E.g., avoid the air-conditioned room at the National Gallery unless you can say that you personally had a hand in mixing the air or advised on the mean warmed-upness. Change the subject and talk instead about something almost completely inaccessible.

"Have you ever seen that little collection at the Walthamstow Waterworks?" you can ask. "Chiefly Saxon, of course, Saxon coins picked out of the King's Scholars' Pond Sewer. The design is de-based Roman, and if you are as absurdly keen on debased Roman as I am, you won't grudge an hour or two at Walthamstow."

Be fairly ruthless, I think, with opponents of "modern" painting. If you are lucky enough to find a man who still says: "I don't know about pictures, but I know what I like," point out to him that be-cause he does not know about pictures he does not know what he likes, and repeat this in a thundering

66

voice. If he whimpers back something about it all being too advanced for him, point out exactly how many years Cézanne died before he was born, and the precise date of the exhibition of the first Modiglianis in London. Exaggerate both these dates and say, "After all, Matisse and your great-grandmother are exact contemporaries." If your man says of some picture, "Yes, but what does it mean?" ask him, and keep on asking him, what his carpet means, or the circular patterns on his rubber shoe-soles. Make him lift up his foot to look at them.

The safest subject for criticism is the accuracy of the descriptive notice. At Kew Gardens it is no bad thing, when wandering through the shades of the collection of elm-tree species, to read out "Ulmus flavescens" from the label and say, "It's not, now, classified as a true elm at all," Or with a display of musical instruments, better still, read out "Violin by Armedio, 1760-1820," and then say, "1760, of course, is complete and utter guesswork."

It is always possible, when in doubt, to "criticise the lack of information for ordinary simple people like myself."

Another useful ploy is to criticise something for what it isn't, even if what it isn't isn't what it is trying to be.

For example, take an exhibition of beautiful books. The basic gambit (since the object of the exhibition is to demonstrate the æsthetic quality of the type, binding, etc.) is to say *plonkingly* that "To me personally a book is something to be read."

You can then pick up three books at random and say of No. 1 that "you'd like to read it if you could see the wood for the trees"; of No. 2 that "the binding is certainly expensive, but does the book fall open *easily and naturally*?" and of No. 3 (*Paradise Lost*, printed in italics) you can say, "Of course, if you like reading poetry at an angle . . . but after ten pages I should be in italics myself." You can raise a laugh by leaning sideways when saying this.[1]

In the same way, at the pottery part of an exhibition it is always possible to say, "What a pity there is no example of Leeds glaze."

When looking at plants or animals in any kind of Natural History show or zoo or gardens just say: "Oh, but it is not the same . . . not the same behind bars." You can say that all round the rock garden at Kew, for instance:

"Pyrenean Iris. Oh yes, yes, yes, but terrible. Terrible if one has ever been overcome by the miracle of this thing bravely clasping the crevice of the perpendicular cliff-face at Luchesse—terrible to see it here, tamed and humbled by man."

I like and recommend this gambit.

Special Exhibition Play.

For crowded buildings and special exhibitions remember, in general, that you are different from the crowd. For instance, if the notice says "TURN

[1] Students must not be confused if, after reading this paragraph, they are left with a feeling that they are not quite certain which side they are meant to be on. If we are continually expected to take sides, that is the end of argument.

LEFT" instantly turn right. Do not trudge round in a crocodile. If there is an injunction to keep moving, stand stock still, eyes fixed on the ceiling.

Again, to suggest that you have the artistically awakened eye and can form your own opinion in perfect independence of the kind of judgment which the lay-out and emphasis of the exhibition seem to demand, pause a long time before some object which has nothing to do with the exhibits—say a fire extinguisher or a grating in the floor through which warmed-up museum air rises—and say, "The influence of William Morris, even here," or just, "Now *that*, to me, is a beautiful object."

The best way to praise the exhibition is to say, "It's a great jaunt, a delightful affair and a huge success. Exhibitions always are a huge success."

You can then criticise.

After showing that you yourself are a jolly and exhibition-minded person, and have enjoyed, in the old days at the White City, the model of the Astronomer Royal in margarine, you can then be generally nasty by complaining that this particular show lacks the indefinable something, the gaiety perhaps, of the Petit Palais Exhibition at Varence in 1931 (designed by Pompipier), or the feeling for Internationalism which one got frightfully from that wonderful Füldenbliegen Collection in the Rond Tor at Uppsala. Behaviouristically, one should be alert and clever, also an expert in exhibition technique. Know, especially if in the company of a varicose aunt, how to park your car three miles away and walk, because it saves time in the end. Know how to come in ten minutes before closing-time, because that is the only way to see the rooms in comfort, if rather quickly. Know how to avoid exhibition malaise, how to diet for exhibitions, and the importance of light salads with a touch of garlic, because the rooms will smell of garlic, anyhow. Know how to keep your mind off what you are looking at, and how to bring pass-the-time puzzles of the kind, for instance, where you separate two twisted nails.

Finally, remember that the best and most overwhelmingly one-up way to go to an exhibition with a person is to be in love with the person and for the person to be in love with you. It is no bad thing to hold hands with the person even if she is not in love with you, so long as she does not look grumpy. It is said, too, that people will instinctively make way for young, or fairly young, lovers. This also puts the exhibition to its right use, as a wooing ground. Experience will suggest how the permanent Exhibitions of London may be utilised. Use as guide Billington's OLD WICKET GATE list (Billington's Woo Aids) of Museum Meeting Grounds.

List entries include a brief description of the kind of girl whom it is suitable to arrange to meet in Room 6 (English Glass) at the V. and A., or the quite different girl you meet by the Beaverbrook at the Tate. And the third type equally distinct in *climate of attraction*, the girl you will meet under the Epstein frieze at the St. James's Park Tube Station.

Don't forget also that there is a fourth type of girl

70

whom you will meet by the east entrance of the Zoo-
logical Gardens. You must use your own judgment
whether to refer, jokingly, to the fact that the cages
for the birds of prey adjoin the turnstile.

FIG. 16. MUSEUMSHIP: CLEARING THE CROWD.
The "All the World Makes Way for Lovers" ploy.

VI

A NOTE ON LITMANSHIP

In a popular American biography of the Founder the following statement occurs: "In tracing the evolution of Gamesmanship, too little stress is placed on Potter's early work The Muse in Chains *(? 1937). For the 'Eng. Lit.' described in the early chapters of this once-forgotten volume, prized item now in book sales, differs little from the Art of Knowing about English Literature Without Actually Reading Any Books—working definition of Litmanship as taught at Yeovil."*

EVERY YEAR HUNDREDS, nay thousands, of young lads and lasses pass through the English Literature courses in the universities of this island. How to help them?

Many students come to us when it is too late, their brains permanently damaged by the dread litticosis. "But I have worked it, worked it out," I once heard a lass of twenty continuously repeating. "If I read all the books I am supposed to read, I shall be 187 years old before I . . . 187 . . ." The rest of the sentence was broken.[1]

Yet ten days later this lass was alert and happy,

[1] "And what about Bandello?" I actually replied, with a grim smile, because we must suppose she was supposed to read the Italian Sources and the sources of the Sources too.

and was leaving our portals, a qualified Lifegirl, to face her Finals Year with new courage. I had noticed how different she looked after attending the first lecture by our Gorboduc Reader, on "First Hand Knowledge My Foot."

Before she left I asked, as she handed over her modest fee, what had particularly helped her.

"Textmanship," she answered, with a shy smile.

Let us give you this one glimpse, then, of what had helped Josephine. Textmanship. How, that is, not only to write an essay[1] about, but *to give detailed comments on the wording* of an examination set book without having actually read it. This is known as Gobbetship.

Gobbetship.

The gobbet, hitherto the bugbear of all examinations in English Literature, is a selection of quotations from a Set Book or Set Text. First we harden students, immunise them, against the intimidating wording of such examination questions. (*"State exactly what you know of the following. Do NOT answer more than SEVEN of the ASTERISKS."*)

Then we teach them what to say. Specimen author, typically, Shakespeare. Specimen play,

[1] Old Yeovillers will understand that in her first lecture Josephine will have been told how to talk about some classic novel—*Wuthering Heights* is taken as type of book student will have heard of but not read—and write about it (*a*) as if she had read all other possible novels of the same type ("Middle Period of the Novel of Passion") or (*b*) as if Brontë was a bit of a copy-cat ("she shows, in her rapid transition from the vast to the intimate, the influence, first, of the literary heirs of *Werther*, second, of the Burney school of domestic observation.")

utterly typically, *Henry IV, Part Two*. Specimen orders: "Annotate the following." Specimen quotation for annotation might be, "The slings and arrows of outrageous fortune," except that this is (*a*) miles too easy, and (*b*) from *Hamlet*. More probably a line like this purposely chosen to put you off:

Who keeps the gate here, ho!

Faced with this ridiculous line, what is the examined Lifeboy to do? All that is necessary is to have read a précis of the plot. Then make use of

1. *The Character Ploy*, and write

One of Shakespeare's subtle touches. Note how even the request for a gate to be opened can reveal the impetuousness of the bluff speaker, the lordly peremptoriness of one accustomed to be obeyed.

Without even knowing the *name* of the speaker, it is possible to go on and on about character, e.g.

This play, full of warriors and their retainers, kings and lords, might be termed a study in the terminology of feudal modes of address.

(Students are recommended to learn above phrase by heart.)

2. *The Compression Ploy*

Quote from the Intro. to your school edition, starting "This line":

This line is typical of Shakespeare's middle-to-late historical period in its compression (essence of poetry).

Earlier, Shakespeare could well have written "What ho!" instead of "Ho!"

3. *Imagery Ploy*

Note how Shakespeare employs metaphors suitable to the soldier or the man "in use of war's account."[1] "Keeps the gate—Keeps the watch" is the imagery of the military man.

4. *Ti-TUM Ti-TUM Ploy*

If you know that a regular blank-verse line is made up of five Ti-TUMS you can look for irregularities such as—here—the start with TUM-ti and say:

Note the reversed stress of the first foot, a rhythmic variation which Shakespeare allowed himself more and more frequently once he freed himself from the bonds of metre.

It is possible to intensify the effect of this rather thin comment by (*a*) being scholarly and referring to 18 per cent. of TUM-ti openings and (*b*) by shooting off some O.K. prose. Thus:

With what gaiety Shakespeare shook off the chains of metre, drawing the fine Toledo blade of his poetic mastery from the rusty scabbard of rules.[2]

It is rather a good thing, in general, to be keen on Shakespeare's freedom from fetters, and when saying that he was not a thin-lipped scholar prying over books, to use

[1] One can soon get the knack of making up Shakespearish quotations like above.
[2] Learn this by heart, too.

5. *The Essentially Theatre Ploy*

and say how bald and inexpressive the line looks *read*, "but speak it and the whole thing leaps to life. Sometimes we forget that *2 Henry IV* was a play, and to be acted."

Fig. 17. "Who Keeps the Gate Here, Ho!"
("Remember it's a play" section.)

It was only when we began to act the line on our little stage that we realised that the words should be spoken outside the door, not inside, as, wrongly, here.

Less recommended and now definitely less O.K., and in fact shelved for a few years, is

6. *The Voice of Shakespeare Ploy*

A pity, because it was always possible to say up to 1925 that any two consecutive words "show Shakespeare's condition at this period." Why, at this time, for instance, "the reiterated suggestion of closed doors and castles, prisons and castellations? Is it not that impending sense of claustrophobic doom and frustration which preceded Shakespeare's tragic period?"

7. *"Shakespeare's Theatre" Ploy*

If by any miracle Lifeboy happens to know that this quotation is the first line of the play, or even if not, he can nowadays do much better than (6) by referring to early inn-yard theatres, upper and lower stages, and the use made of them in such a line as this.

Finally 8. *Punctuation Ploy*

Point out that there is no proof that the punctuation is Shakespeare's and if it was (?) instead of (!) or especially (!!) at the end of the line, the whole sense would be changed. This is good gambiting. Super gambiting is to show you are

9. *Versed in the Language of Shakespeare and his Contemporaries.*

and go on like this:

Who . . . here, ho! "Who" is here, I think, the indefinite (= "He who"), and not the interrogative pronoun, as is implied, for instance, by the punctuation, "Who keeps the gate here? ho!" (*Oxford Shakespeare*), and "Who keeps the gate here, ho?" (*Cambridge Shakespeare*). "Who keeps the gate" is a periphrasis (= "Porter") of a kind usual in calling to servants or others, in attendance but out of sight. Cf. *Henry VIII.* V.ii.2, 3: *"Cran . . .*

Ho! Who waits there!" Cf. also Beaumont and Fletcher, *Maid's Tragedy*, V.iii: "*Lys* . . . Summon him, Lord Cleon. *Cleon.* Ho, from the walls there!" and *Jack Straw* (Hazlitt's *Dodsley*, V.396): "Neighbours, you that keep the gates."

This last gambit, shortened by two-thirds from Lifemanship's Arden Edition of Shakespeare, needs training, even if every single reference is made up. It is not known whether the above are.

L.C.C. POST-GRADUATE

Some Simple Uses of Litmanship

1. ARE YOU FOND OF READING?

I like to finish these sections with examples of our applied instruction for post-graduates.

What is the use, Litmen are often asked, of being able to read Chaucer's *Prologue* in the original if you don't know what to do with it in after life? It is precisely in such a Life-situation as this that we like to feel we can be of most use.

Well Readship.

In a word, how to appear well read. How to make it appear, without giving books more than a casual glance, for surely there is not time, that no man is quicker than yourself off the mark with the latest thriller, newest white paper on the development of opencast tungsten mining, or most recent reminiscences of some unheard-of nephew of Dante Gabriel Rossetti.

Coad-Sanderson was always my model here, and

it was I who created him our Longfellow Reader at
L.C.C. He ate, drank and slept the new books.
Wall-paper controller, with income of £720 p.a.,
and a mother and stepmother to support, as well as
his stepmother's stepchildren, Coad could afford
to buy very few books indeed. His methods were and
are: (1) To collect book jackets from a peaceful
reviewer, Horton, whom he knows and who helps
him. These jackets he wraps round old books so
that his library seems to be in a constantly refreshed
and up-to-date state. He has also (2) beautifully
developed the technique of Upright Reading—that
is to say, perusing books in bookshops without
actually buying them.[1] He also (3) reads the kind of
review which enables you to criticise a book without
having actually read it, and finally (4) he keeps

[1] The fact that Coad hardly read the books he possessed or that
these were few in number was never revealed. Coad was himself
deeply influenced by the brilliant specialisations of (Miss) S. Arnold-
Forster on Marginaliaship and the ! Ploy. Miss Arnold-Forster has
perfected a means of suggesting to borrowers of books that their
reading is superficial and that they are imperceptive of the finer
nuances. This is done by underlinings, comments, etc., written on
the margins of the book at random *in ink*.

"Surely" ploy:

"At this time William Cowper had at last settled down with his
old nurse and six cats at Bath, in the house he had so recently
bought."

Question-mark ploy:

"It might be said that Wordsworth's childhood in the Lakes
may have profoundly influenced his poetic development."

Exclamation-mark ploy:

"Maria Edgeworth's early experiences in the Liverpool slums
brought home to her that drink is indeed an evil mocker, and she
remained a total abstainer all her life."

certain blocks of typewritten manuscript always on show and will sometimes say, "Willie Maugham allowed me to browse through this before he made the final corrections. There was little I could say which was of any value to him, I fear."

It might be supposed that Coad-Sanderson, in order to maintain his gambit, would have to read fifteen books a week.

He was saved from this stupefying task by two strong sub-qualifications, as we call them. The first: Coad was an Old Reviewer himself. He knew that there are only six things which can under any conceivable circumstances be said for, not more than eight to be said against, any known book.[1]

---

[1] Not only O.K. Literary Names, with Rilking (see *Lifemanship*, p. 78), are taught at L.C.C., but basic O.K. critical phrases (with intonations) as well. No matter if they tell us very little of the object to be criticised; the main function is to imply ("I'm Rather Delightfulship") that you, the critic, are an extraordinarily nice chap. E.g.

O.K. critical lines:

    (1) "Thank goodness there's no mention of Freud"

or

    "Personally I'm sick of the Oedipus complex" (there need not, of course, be any reference to Freud or complexes in the work concerned).

    (2) "Delightfully fresh and spontaneous."

Both (1) and (2) will suggest that the critic, in spite of his rather scruffy appearance, *is himself pretty fresh and spontaneous.*

    (3) "A rewarding experience."

("Rewarding" is the new O.K. word for 1952. "Climate of thought" is still O.K., but only just. "Rebarbative" is *finito*).

O.K. Attacks:

    (4) "Personally I found the love-scenes rather embarrassing."

    (5) "There is a certain archness which I found displeasing."

It is also possible, within eleven minutes, to learn five words to quote (supposed to be a certain way of proving that you have read the book through). Remember that any five consecutive words taken out of *any dramatic* passage of a novel or *deeply passionate* section of a poem will sound both forced and absurd if repeated by you on the top of a tram, while mixing a drink, or while the person you are speaking to is filling up a form.

If by chance one happened actually to have read a book on the morning of publication, Coad could always go one better. I have myself rushed round to Coad with a copy of, say, T. D. Pontefract's *The Tea Party* at 11 o'clock—two hours after it was issued—to see if I could for once be one up on him over a new book. I do not remember what he said, but experience has taught me it must have been either (*a*) "Let me lend you the American edition. It's beautifully printed and it hasn't got that stupid cut on page 163," or (*b*) (more simply) "Good old Pontefract—still churning them out."

This answer (*b*) brings me to the second sub-qualification which made things more possible for

---

(4) and (5) mean "*Though sensitive and cultured, my peasant stock ensures that I am O.K. for passion.*"

(6) Quote misquotations of commas.

(7) Complainingly quote clichés, or at any rate say, "Why must 'blood' always be 'congealed'? " as if it *was* a cliché.

(8) In criticising any translation, take any five lines of the translation and then quote the original and say, "Why not let's have the original, so much more force and point, etc." If the original language is Syriac, so much the less chance of argument.

Coad in his pursuit of Keeping Abrcastmanship. There are latest books and latest books, he would imply; and after he reached the age of forty-four, when reading became even more difficult for him, he would make a tremendous point, though as up to date as ever, of only buying the books "which interested him."

"Look, I've got a prize," he would say to me. "I've got it too," said I breathlessly, pointing to my new Julius Simon.

"Ah, good, good," Coad says now. "But I didn't actually mean that one. Where does the Mysterious Religious Character come in this time? Chapter XIV?"

This maddened me, (a) because I had in fact been rather moved by Chapter XIV, and (b) because I knew Coad was going to pull out some small, almost privately printed book and say, "I meant this— John's new book on the architecture of lift shafts. It's most frightfully good."

I have said sufficient, I think, to show Coad's gambit. And what, you will say, of the counter? For each ploy has its anti. Coad is counter-proof, but there is a way of making the average newbook-man feel feeble. It is based on a remark made 125 years ago next March by that domineering Lifeman Charles Lamb.

Lamb said, when any of his friends bought a new book, he bought an old one. This, in my view, is difficult to beat, as a ploy. There is an answer to it. Play can be made with the period flavour of ivorytowership, as a gambit. Yet on the whole it is a reasonably disabling ploy, and the only reason we sometimes frown on it is that, containing as it does a grain of truth, the taste remaining in the mouth is scarcely a pleasant one.[1]

[1] *Wilson's Wile.*
We are working now on the counter to this ploy of J. Wilson of Oxford Street, i.e. the bookseller's ploy of knowing more about the subject than the author who has written the book on it.

Fig. 18. "Receiving Day."

A group of us ready to welcome the new batch of week-end "guests." On the left, Odoreida, with Cogg-Willoughby in characteristic pose. On the right, Ivy Spring and Gattling-Fenn.

PART TWO
THE HOUSE PARTY
ORIGIN OF THE HOUSE PARTY

The title "Lifemaster"—what does it mean, what does it stand for?

In the old days it stood for a thorough course at the Life-manship College, including such extras as Foreign Languaging and Manglo-Relations. These were not optional. The test was severe. Credits were necessary in eighteen of the twenty-two subjects, and the candidates must have satisfied the examiners in at least one of the papers of London Matriculation.

But there were many promising students who found this insistence on mere scholastic ability a permanent bar to high office. A profession where personality was so important needed a new test. It was for this purpose that the House Party was created. It is an institution copied now, I am glad to report, very honourably, we need not say by whom, and familiar throughout the British Army in the technique and counter-techniques of Wosbyship.

In essence our House Party is a friendly enough affair, in which young Lifemen visit us as guests (for list of fees see back page of pamphlet) and are made to feel uneasy, but not aggressively so, while they on their part make their student attempts to undermine our long-trained one-upness.

We watch our candidates, of course, without their knowing it, although they are all aware of this being watched without knowing it. As they drive the car or wield rod or gun, field-glass or wine-glass, qualities of Lifeleadership and the reverse are quickly spotted. Few may there be to fail to be awarded the title, with its additional fee, of Lifemaster.

VII

THE CARMANSHIP OF
GODFREY PLASTE

SOMETIMES THE LIFEMASTER candidate at the House Party is under inspection before he realises it.

Take, for instance, the journey down, by train or car. Perhaps he will have some lifetutor as companion. If in a car, he is supposed to know something of car theory, and to have read our pamphlet, here reproduced in shortened form, on *Carmanship: or the art of stealing the crown of the road without being an absolute hog*.

Godfrey Plaste, our Differential Reader in Carmanship and for many years referee at our Gameslife Students' Sportsground, must have written nearly a third of a million words on the various Lifemanship gambits associated with his almost too passionate spare-time interest in car and driver play. Never satisfied, Plaste tore up sheet after sheet as he wrote, sometimes even before, until at last only four complete pages remained. These he handed over, with a rather fulsome dedication, to myself, expressing a hope that I would not publish.

As this "wish" was obviously only a gambit, now that Plaste has passed on I am giving what I hope is the gist of Plaste's pages here, trying as it were to reconstruct from the fourth lumbar vertebra, the skeleton of a Plasteploy.

As is admitted, Godfrey's motor play evolved from one primary gambit which he perfected over many years. It is known—easy phrase to remember—as "Plaste's Placid Salutation," and I am bound to say he brought this to a fine art.

FIG. 19. PLASTE'S PLACID SALUTATION.

A ferociously selfish driver, Plaste gloried in bringing approaching limousines to a dead stop by choosing the wrong moment to overtake. I have myself seen an on-coming quadruple tank-carrier forced by Plaste's carefully timed passing to mount the verge and melt through a concrete lamp-standard. Yet Plaste got away with it by this "salutation." In essence this was a simple raising of the hand, an inclination of the head, and a grave smile. Instead of the scream of rage one would expect from the oncomers, they would often *actually salute back*.

Why was this? The only time I met Plaste on the road head-on he was passing an ambulance. Notic-ing the ambulance bell, I had slowed down and pulled well over. It was one of the narrowest two-lane traffic sections of the notorious Great North Road. Suddenly the light blue nose of Plaste's battered little saloon, screaming in some low gear, crept out behind. I almost drove the brakes through the floor. As my head hit the windscreen, I saw the hand raised slowly in salute.

There was something so calm and dignified about this gesture that I can only say that instead of anger I was made to feel that I had somehow helped; that some message of urgency for the nation had passed that way, a second saved, a crisis averted. I am not sure that I didn't salute back. It was only afterwards, looking back and recognising the honeycomb of dents on the mudguards of Plaste's wretched car, that I became angry, and slowly began to shout.

It was the success of this gambit of his which set Plaste thinking in terms of carmanship.

Ever since he was a child he has been fascinated by Back-seat Drivership (the Beastly Passenger ploy), a palæo-gambit which existed before Gamesmanship and Yeovil were thought of. Plaste's passenger technique was first to remain absolutely silent for five or six minutes. Then a long time before it was necessary for me to brake he would fidget with his

FIG. 20. PLASTE AS PASSENGER (from an X-ray photograph).

We were fortunate to obtain this record of the position of Plaste's right foot, made at the moment when, using the Lifeman's "art which reveals art" (Morteroy), he "instinctively" brakes as his driver approaches a roundabout. Note particularly the flexure—almost a flexion—of Distal and Middle Phalanges, to suggest that driver's speed is carelessly excessive.

feet, but slightly. Later, when it was known that I
should have to turn left, he would stretch his left arm
far out of the car, half a mile before the turning-
point; and for a right turn jig his extended hand up
and down as if he were scrambling eggs, thus making
a dangerous Highway Code error and at the same time
suggesting that my hand signals were ineffective.

If we approached a child under the age of twelve
walking quietly along the footpath, he would first
wince, then draw up his knees, then say, "Toot toot"
quietly under his breath.

PLASTE: Toot-toot.
SELF: What did you say?
PLASTE: Only "toot-toot" . . . I wasn't quite sure
whether you'd seen that child on the footpath.
SELF (*pause*): But it's walking into the house.
PLASTE: *Oo*—yes. All right now. Exquisite little
thing.

But if the tables were turned and he was driving,
Plaste had amazing powers of making his passengers
feel beastly. If, after dashing at full speed across
three dangerous crossings, he was about to emerge,
as he once was, I remember, from Wallingford on to
the main Oxford road in Henley Week, I did say,
smiling, "By the way, major road ahead." Plaste
stopped his car instantly, drawing it into the side.

"Look," he said. "Do you mind if I tell you something? I have been driving a car for twenty-five
years, and if any passenger is going to tell me what
to do he brings to the realm of the conscious the very
thing which experience has happily made intuitive

and natural. I do not mind bad manners, but I do mind death. Thank you." Of course what he said was absolutely right, and as he dashed out into the Oxford road and tipped off his front wing against a beer lorry, I began to mumble apologies.

"Forget it," he said to me.

Plaste had another method of "softening" his passengers. He had in his locker a collection of out-of-date and crumpled maps made at very different dates to very different scales, and through long wear rubbed into illegibility round the creases. He would hand a bunch of these to me and say, "How about a little map-reading?" After ten minutes finding the right map and another ten finding the right place, Plaste would say, "I say, do you mind keeping that map in the right folds?"

"Yes," I said—really slightly pulling his leg. Then after another two minutes:

"Well?" he would say.

"What do you mean, 'Well?'?" I would say.

"Where are we?"

"Getting on," I said. (I knew we were about half-way between Nettlebed and Henley.)

Plaste began to use his quiet voice: "Yes, yes, but I mean where are we? I mean, it makes it so much more interesting."

"We're not anywhere exactly."

"What do you—I wonder what that rather jolly little wood over there is called?"

After about three minutes' twisting and turning of the map I reply, "It says 'Upper Common.' "

Plaste would then irritate me by using the annoying word "Folkmoot" and saying, "Doesn't that touch your imagination? Perhaps on this Common Land the Folkmoot was once held; the clearing in the forest."

With women map-readers Plaste was even quieter and more incisive. He would say very clearly and slowly, "All set, my dear? Now look, we want the second third-class road to the left."

"To the left on the map?" most women would reply. "How do you mean?" Plaste would say, rather charmingly. Then: "Are you orientated?"

After a pause the woman might say, "Won't there be a signpost?" To this Plaste replied, "What?" Still smiling, he would make elaborate hand signals and draw in to the side. "I expect we've overshot it, haven't we? Let's see if I can find the place."

After four or five minutes of this, few women could tell the difference between a railway line and a reservoir, and there would be one of those lapses into tearful silence which satisfied Plaste so much.

This, I hope, will give the student what may be called Plaste definitive. For the rest, it is a scribbled note here, a word-of-mouth tradition there. Godfrey ployed his last ploy three years ago sadly enough, self-gambited. A collision while driving in reverse.

How did this come about? One of Plaste's most feverishly irritating techniques, we are told, was his knowledge-of-Londonship. He would go a whole mile off route to wind his way through some goods yard because it was the "only way of avoiding the

Notting Hill traffic." To complain that this would not affect your journey to Swiss Cottage, anyhow, would be to play into Plaste's hands. He would "know some parking place" under a disused railway bridge only accessible by taxi. He would know "definite spots in parks where there could be no speed trap" and use his information by speeding at 50 m.p.h. round and round the Victoria Monument outside Buckingham Palace, for instance—quite useless of course. Finally, and fatally, Plaste would always approach one-way streets from the wrong end and then go up them backwards. "Saves time," he said.[1] It was while performing this evolution that he reversed at 30 m.p.h. into a car which was approaching in the correct direction at a similar speed.

Too late, alas, for Plaste to leap out of his car, his usual practice when he hit somebody, and cry "Did you get that man's number?" We have the Plaste car in our Yeovil museum, though it is not usually on show. Not of any make, it was originally put together from spare parts by C. Plaste, G. Plaste's nephew, son of V. Plaste, the iron-railing manufacturer. The bonnet looked feebler than nine horses, but beneath it was, in fact, an old 17-h.p. engine with six cylinders, noisy enough, but impressive when "G. P." slipped into third and said "Not bad for nine horses."

[1] Having spent nine months' practice in backing, this one branch of his driving was good, and as a wooman Plaste managed to keep one girl faithful to him for 2½ years by constantly demonstrating his virtuosity in reverse.

The engine pinked like a chime of bells. "Must do," said Plaste proudly, "with this little tiger, built for hotted-up aviation spirit." In the back of the car is the string of tin medals out of crackers which Plaste referred to as "Médailles d'Honneur Club Belgique." There on the back seat are the tyre chains with special spikes for the Courboise Pass . . . Monte Carlo Rally."[1] On the dash of his car, examine the starter button, which is a dummy. Plaste would press this useless button, and then say, "Never mind, half a jiff."

I can see him now, whisking out three adjustable spanners, and then his long pink bony wrists would disappear under the bonnet where the normal starter button was concealed. "Got it," he would say, as the engine miraculously leapt into action, while the female passenger exclaimed with admiration at what appeared to be a miracle of mechanical comprehension, deftness and male mastery. There is no Plaste Memorial, but the simple, common nettles along the west side of our sports ground have remained uncut. He would have wished it so.

---

[1] I have been asked in the preparation of this book to insert a footnote on the Monte Carlo Rally, or Rallyship,[1] as I prefer to call it. As I myself go in for a different type of dangerous driving, I am in process, through conversations, of stabilising the rules of Rallyship with Carlo One (R. Walkerley) who is in close touch with many fellow drivers at the Carburettor Club, which maintains its delightful atmosphere of incomprehensibly technical gambiting. Thus (at random):

A: Last Saturday!—
B: What?

---

[1] This footnote is highly technical, and should be read only by those who have achieved some record time round some record track. We ourselves hold a record for Silverpebble, having lapped it at 14 m.p.h. in an unblown Bean.

A: You were fairly streaking along at Bedtimber.

B: Oh, I don't know. We dropped 900 revs on the second lap—just as you passed me.

A: Did I pass you—no, you were Number Ten, weren't you? I'd got my eyes so glued on the tail of Farina . . .

Rallyman A wins, with his suggestion that he was only really concerned with super-ace rivals.

The Carburettor Club has its own set of ploys belonging to what they term the Dicing-with-Death group or Dicemanship. Here are the two basic approaches, nicknamed the Walkerley Talkerleys.

DICEMAN A: Actually I was petrified. No anchors whatever, after two laps, so I suppose I did go rather fast round those corners. Actually, I was a bit shaken.

DICEMAN B: I know. But for some unearthly reason it seems to go the other way with me. You know that little Silverpebble incident when I lost a wheel? I went sort of calm and rather cold. I seemed to have bags of time to pull up on the grass, get out and walk away. But, lord, was I scared, later, when I thought about it!

Here is a parlette of Drink-diceman, interesting if only because it gives a perfect example of the riposte or anti-counter:

A: Drink?

B: No thanks. Got to drive on Saturday.

A: Well, speaking absolutely personally, I'm scared to get into the car unless I'm practically completely stinkaroo. (*He roars with laughter.*)

This is good ploying, as everybody thinks that A, who has built up an atmosphere of never drinking anything but Coco-Cola, is amusing and decent. Everybody, that is, but B, who knows that A always uses private flask before race.

VIII

THE CARTER-WILLIAMS
RAILWAY GAMBITS

"I know Carter-Williams personally," said a young House Party guest to me one Friday, hoping to impress as he stepped out not of a car but the third-class compartment of a railway carriage, holding a first-class ticket in his hand. I approved of his sound railway-ticket play, with its suggestion of affluence devoid of snobbery; but I had to pull him up on "Carter-Williams."

"*Which do you mean?*" I said, for of course B. Carter and J. Williams, though known to each other, are two totally distinct persons, young National Service men who as sergeants were expert in furloughship, as we used to call it, and studied railwayship over a prolonged period of leave-fiddling. Far apart in conveyed climate as each terminus is, the Eustonian and Paddingtonian approaches are basically similar, at the deepest level.[1]

There is, of course, one essential railway gambit in which each student is supposed to perfect himself.

[1] "The Underground is the Great Leveller" was first said by the amazing John Stuart Mill *at the age of four*, only 2½ years after he first mastered the Greek alphabet. Some part of our Fifth Volume, 1956, will be devoted to precocityship and its counter, Miltoning, sometimes defined as the art of not writing *Paradise Lost* before fifty.

But before reminding you of this, which always comes at the close of our railway pamphlet, a reminder of Cogg-Willoughby and his railway work.

Cogg has only one railway gambit, and it is simple. It is to use the railway.

"I never go by car," he says. "Goodness no."

So even, say, between Redhill and Dorking, he will take the frightfully old-fashioned electrified rail system. Portsmouth to London by rail is typical Cogg. And his total effect, of course, is to be alone, to be clean, especially about the finger-nails, to be unruffled, to read, and to go first-class with a third-class ticket—the reverse of the procedure we normally recommend. He also uses a cigarette-holder —quite unlike his normal character this—but effec-

FIG. 21. THE BASIC RAILWAYSHIP OF COGG.

Note: the book is Ruskin's *Seven Lamps*. The names of other books can be supplied.

tive, I am bound to say, with his thin discriminating temples and the vulnerable effect of his prematurely bald head. He wears horn-rimmed glasses designed by Chermayeff and *gloves while reading*.

He is usually sitting alone, occasionally non-smoking in a smoker, nice touch. And always quite clean, and calm. All this is aimed, need we say, at the Gattling-Fenns of this world.

Gattling, door to door, can get there seven minutes faster, over the 2¼-hour journey, by plunging through wind and traffic in his white-and-green roadster. But whereas Gattling on arrival is nervy, dishevelled and half his normal size with the desire for drink, Cogg-Willoughby steps out of his taxi ironed and tidied, and poisedly asks for soda-water.

But to return to Carter-Williams. As young militiamen they made great game, on long-distance journeys with dining-cars, of pretending to have dinner on both the first and second service while really eating sandwiches or even nothing, and vice versa—a lot of horseplay, to my mind.

But they did pick up a surprising amount of railship lore, and made a few converts with their slapdash slogan—BE TOP MAN—WIN THE JOURNEY.

Little Wootton Play.

Superior knowledge of the route was one method.[1] ("Little Wootton Play" is the random naming of

[1] To describe Method Two I will quote direct from Carter:
"On the first reference by any of his travelling companions to the heat or stuffiness of the compartment J. Williams would leap to his feet, open all the windows and the door into the corridor, and *turn*

indecipherable stations after they have flashed by.) In the dark at speed I have myself found it possible to convince passengers that I know the position of the train *by sounds*. I say:

SELF: That loop of the Ouse is on our right now. (No need to say which of the fourteen Ouses you are referring to.)

PASSENGER: How on earth do you know?

SELF: That rattle of points and then the rap as we went under the footbridge. Cobb's Corner.

FIG. 22. RAILWAYSHIP: LITTLE WOOTTON PLAY.

During dark, nod towards any small lighted window as it passes and say, "Ah, Tom's in—Tom Norris, head keeper of Lord Gravelstoke in the old days."

Actually this patter was used against me by the dignified driver of the Coronation Scot. It was only afterwards that I discovered there was no footbridge and no Ouse.

At the end of their pamphlet, Carter-Williams describe Rail Primary—the gambit we all practise yet never perfect. And how often in fact we fail in —what? In *Terminus Technique*.

---

the heating off. He would then put on coat, gloves and muffler, and wait."

The counter-ploy to this, of course, is to take off your jacket, loosen your collar, and *appear to enjoy* the fresh air. But this move has never been used since *Healthman's Disaster*, when two determined Lifemen, travelling on the Flying Scotsman, arrived in Edinburgh frozen, almost incredibly, to death.

FIG. 23.   TERMINUS PLAY.
The seated figure is in the correct Eustonian position.
(*Sketch made while passing Watford on the up line.*)

There are still men, albeit the layest of the lay, who, coming into Euston, will begin fidgeting even before Watford, say "Are we here?" begin to button some sort of dingy macintosh, take down suitcase and remain standing, meaninglessly. "New boy," we all intone at him in a repeated plainsong—but are we always perfect ourselves?

Let me quote Carter:

If you are truly established as Top Man, your fellow-passengers will leave you to judge the correct moment.

There are two methods :

1. The Eustonian. If the line is well-known to you, as terminus approaches sit absorbed in a book, and make no preparations for disembarkation until *the very last minute*. Long practice in our Yeovil dummy railway carriage makes it possible to snap book shut and get out smoothly precisely as train stops.

2. The Paddingtonian. If you do not know line well enough to employ (1), act as follows. Prepare to leave the train *at least half an hour* before you are likely to reach your destination. Then leave compartment with word about "getting opposite taxi." Lay passengers are left feeling gloomy, apprehensive and feeble.

IX

GAME BIRDSMANSHIP

DURING THE FIRST day of our Yeovil week-end we
encourage candidates to get out and about, either
playing games according to methods recommended
by us or taking part in sports, often called the
"shipless" sports because hitherto nothing has been
printed by us on these themes.[1]

But now the time has come to get down on paper
some basic code for shooting, fishing, etc., encouraging our Yeovil demonstrators[2] in each subject to
say something of their technique.

Gifted Colonel F. Wilson, illustrator of our
manuals, and often quite welcome when an extra
beater is wanted, is Purdey Reader in Game
Birdsmanship and avers that the whole craft needs
a thorough spring-cleaning.

We are certainly cutting out, I hope, a good deal

[1] Nothing printed but plenty talked. For three years shooting men
of all denominations, yes and fishermen too, have been sending in
messages, "advise" here, "pronounce" there. "Coarse Fishermen
Expect a Lead from Yeovil" is a headline some may have seen in the
journalism of this sport.

[2] These sporting-life demonstrators are not on the regular Yeovil
staff nor are they permanent. The post is held for one year during
which three lectures are given somewhere or other, often in the Off-
Licence of some tavern. The office is known as Morning Dew
Reader, although being able to read is neither essentially required
nor an invariable acquirement. There is no special interest in this.

FIG. 24. GAME BIRDSMANSHIP: BECKETT'S BALK.

M. Beckett's suggested technique for grouse shooting. Host
sends guests to next line of butts in cars across bumpy track while he
rides direct on old and sure-footed pony.

A   B

FIG. 25. UNSTEADYING EFFECT OF BECKETT'S BALK.
A. Guest.   B. Host.

of dead wood. The man who trains his dog to go
out quick after the drive and pick birds indiscrimin-
ately from all the way down the line—this man is no
gamesman and should not so name himself.[1] And

[1] Away, too, with the man who says, "Care to try my 'Superstrike?'
Knock over an elephant at a hundred
yards" and hands his unsuspecting guest
a cartridge filled not with normal charge
but ordinary toy "caps" for children.

there is something, too, like boasting even about Gattling-Fenn's reply to his host's complimentary "You must have got over twenty birds there":

"No, only nineteen came."

A good deal of Game-birding work has been done recently on the subject of luncheon in butt or by hedgerow.

Gattling and Cogg-Willoughby are contrasted here. Cogg goes in for especially luxurious luncheon-hampers, better than anybody else's, with special instruments, e.g. for cracking the shells of hard-boiled eggs. Gattling contrastingly produces a tin of hambones with only a few rags of ham left and some dog biscuits. His object (he tells students) is to show how absolutely at one he is with his dog. "He is part of me," says Gattling. Whenever his dog, Fossil, does anything (scratches, takes a left turn, etc.) Gattling will say at the same moment something like "Huppah" and add "You see," as if what the dog did was the result of his saying "Huppah." After opening the dog biscuits Gattling sometimes

Fig. 26. Gattling-Fenn Developing Dogmanship to the Point of Absurdity.

104

went off with Fossil to drink and even lap water at the same horse-trough. So much interest was soon aroused by these goings on that people on the fringe of our group would be offering Gattling chicken sandwiches or even inexpensive champagne, so that he always ended by getting a better lunch than anybody.

"How do you do it?" I heard a Mrs. Ems ask Gattling, admiring his dog's obedience.

"Just patience," said Gattling. "Patience. And being rather fond of the creatures."

This annoyed me because I knew that Fossil privately loathed Gattling, and the only objects Fossil could and did pick up effectively were golf balls in play, usually from the first fairway of Huntercombe Golf Course.

One basic we can reveal as emerging in our Yeovil teaching, and that is that clothesmanship for game birdsmen *is perhaps more important than in any other sport*.

I do not wish to publish details of this yet, but would like to draw attention to a gambit of F. Wilson's own, with which we are all particularly wont to associate him personally here, although the "official" name for the gambit is cumbersome ("Wilson's Wali of Swatship"). Its object is to suggest supershot one-upness by reference to first-hand knowledge of jungle sport, if not warfare.

"Nice bit of jungle," is Wilson's opening line.

Wilson's next move is to handle his gun in a way which companion finds strange though not yet alarming.

WALIMAN: "Sorry, I'm not used to this."

LAYMAN: "Oh, well."

WALIMAN: "I mean I'm not used to shooting with other people. I used to go out alone. Quite alone. Except of course for a few natives. It didn't matter if you peppered them."

LAYMAN: "Of course."

WALIMAN: "They liked it because I used to put an anna over each little skin puncture. Sometimes they used to *pretend* to be knocked out."

FIG. 27.
WILSON'S BLOOD-STAINED ANNA.

It was in really cold weather that one saw the perhaps rather hateful side of this Far Eastern play. Wilson would wear a warm-looking sheepskin Afghanistan coat or poshteen. From the nice-chap approach Wilson would then offer other poshteens to fellow guns. "Can't do anything with cold fingers."

Wrongly fitted or put on, however, these coats have a trussing-up effect quite fatal, of course, to good shooting. By doing up a certain button, Wilson made wearers feel as if they had been skewered through the armpits. Then Wilson would say: "The Wali of Swat gave me this. I don't know why . . . we sort of hit it off. He laid on a fifteen-gun salute for me. Frightful brigand of course. Here, let me pull this out of your eyes."

FIG. 28. GAME BIRDSMANSHIP IN OXON.
The Wilson Strait-jacket.

"This" would refer to the Yarkandi hat which Wilson provided as an extra. With its wide, loose fur rim it would gradually settle on to the bridge of the nose.

Odoreida was such a bad shot that he could only get himself invited by some stratagem or forgery. Little to report on him, except this variation on the Striking Stranger gambit (see *Lifemanship*, p. 114).

I have always said that Odoreida was repulsive to women: but be that as it may, women were certainly repulsive to him, with the exception of his rather dolphin-breasted sister-in-law Paulette Odoreida, at whom he did once make a somewhat hectoring

FIG. 29. GAME BIRDSMANSHIP IN NORFOLK.

Mrs. Paulette Odoreida distracting. The colour of her scarf is canary.

kind of pass. He even made ploy with this quite handsome woman and her two young friends, asking if he might bring them to a shoot. Once there, he would leave these youngish women embarrassingly alone, so that other guns would have to carry them over ditches or prize apart barbed-wire fences with a testy show of chivalry.

Odoreida trained Paulette to wear a gay light yellow scarf and then sit by the butt of a rival. Ocular reflexes caused the birds to turn aside out of range.

Remember, finally, the importance of the "I'm not just a slayer" approach to this subject, with the man who is interested in the natural history of the thing well in the foreground. But this subject needs a new chapter, and a new guide.

X

BIRD GAMESMANSHIP

THE ORIGIN OF Bird Gamesing, or Bearded Tit-manship, is easy to guess. The whole vast ornitho-ploy started as a natural-history gambit of ordinary game-bird shooting (see last chapter). It was Gilbert White, when out with his friend D. Barrington taking pot-shots at cuckoos, who first said, "Yes, but how does it rear its young?" after which Barrington never hit a bird.

Our Zeiss Reader is B. Campbell, who, even if he was unlucky enough to be sacked from Selborne, still writes actual bird notes in ornithological papers. The essence of this Birdsmanship he explains in a large work, which will be divided into three volumes.

The first volume will deal with *The Birdsman in Society* and the two basic ways of making the layman feel ill at ease. We have adapted these for Yeovil as follows:

1. In answer to Layman's respectful question to Birdsman, "Do tell me, is this a good place for birds?" answer "Well, no place is bad for birds really, is it?" This is said in an anti-plonking or softly sym-pathetic voice with a touch of substitute Richard Jefferies,[1] or at any rate a "Let me be your Fabre" hint, always annoying.

[1] Hence the term "Jefferiesship" for this put-off.

2. A totally contrasted method can be used for Layman's "Ah, you might be interested about my robin." Without moving a muscle, say, "Certainly, so long as you're not going to tell me that it (*a*) taps on your window or (*b*) really recognises you."

This completes the first volume.

"But what do you mean—a whole volume?" newcomers ask.

"Yes."

"But isn't it rather meagre?"

The newcomer is ignorant of the scientific approach. The good birdsman can always fill up by saying whether or not pocket handkerchiefs were worn by which speaker and if so was it used or if it wasn't and other observations especially absolutely unselected because once you start selecting and therefore expressing preferences the scientific attitude and the whole value of the thing as evidence goes bang. But Vol. II is certainly more important. The Birdsman in the Field.

Binocular Play.

Basic Birdsman is of course to have the best pair of field-glasses in any group. What we teach is the counter to this gambit, the familiarity of which has bred contempt. Method A is to say, "There comes a point, I suppose, when if they're too big and cumbrous you can't get them on the bird quickly enough." Counter B is the man who keeps a very small telescope up his trouser leg.

It is worth remembering, we think, that bad old

binoculars fit well into bird clothesmanship, which surely must consist, basically, as Campbell suggests, in wearing the oldest remains of *two* plus-four suits, bound or patched with leather in unusual places, and a hat which before wearing has been left for a week in a chicken-run.

FIG. 30.
BIRD CLOTHESMANSHIP BASIC.

Above: Classic type.

Below: Modern type, still in experimental stages.

Bearded Titmanship.

This is the name given to the art of being in essence one-up in the art of spotting uncommon birds.[1] Rivalry in this kind of field-work is intense and many a broken nose results, while the words "bigot" or "sewer-rat" are flung back and forth in the correspondence columns of *The Times.*

[1] Don't, for heaven's sake, say "rare." A bird is only rare if it was "reported over Sheppey in 1908 and one shot by Colonel Westrup in Mull in 1884." No, the rare birds you are looking for, such as the bearded tit, are either "infrequent" or "local."

Campbell-recommended parlettes are as follows:

(*a*) In the case of a not readily identifiable bird that stays put, birdsman *must* be the first to ask, "Well, what do you think?" which gives him the chance of trapping an unwary diagnosis from his rival. Should this agree with his own private opinion, he jumps in with: "Of course, but the superciliary stripe (or absence of super-ciliary stripe) was a bit unexpected, wasn't it?"

Alternatively,

(*b*) "I never think it's safe to diagnose at this time of year unless one can see the wing-pattern"

is quite good.

Tallyship has its own disciples and converts. It consists of keeping tally of the number of species observed in one garden, walk, week-end, or hovering over the funnel of the *Bournemouth Queen*. Adepts in this gambit have achieved high virtuosity (recommended method: walk through e.g. a wood head down and whenever some animal lets out some sort of squeak make mark in notebook and say e.g. "nuthatch".) But if tallymen can scarcely be outdone, they can sometimes be made to feel they are doing the wrong thing.

Play the opposite line. To undercut tallyman and bearded titman by one simple counterploy, show a sudden liking for watching quite plain and ordinary birds.

"After all, it's only the common birds that really count, isn't it?" Continually hold up the party by calling their attention to robins or hedge-sparrows sitting in huddled attitudes on the vegetation. If after five minutes' observation the robin gives a perfunctory peck at its plumage, say, "Nice—an intention movement!" and make notes.

Bird Committeeship.

Campbell's third volume will be devoted to Bird Gamesmanship committee meetings, to the use of a pipe[1] at meetings, and to the art of suddenly saying,

[1] Mention of the use of the pipe in scientific argument and indeed in committee work generally reminds me of the pioneer work on pipemanship of E. Sigsworth of Leeds University (*Yeovil Post-Graduate Research*, Vol. CIV, p. 86), "If you have no advice to give, the pipe will do it for you"—how often has this been said: but Sigsworth, with his addition of the technique of spittlecraft to the pipeworthy situation, has put order into the chaos of "intuitive" pipe behaviour.

To give an impression of dependable listening, it is essential to known *when* to puff smoke, when to go "bup" or "bp" with the lips, and when to take a long noisy wet-sounding blow through an extinguished pipe, to clear the passage.

We usually practise on some young woman who wishes to talk to us in confidence—usually about some love affair. Here is a timed table of pipe effects, with dialogue:

GIRL: . . . and I've often wondered whether I was right to make friends with him even. He would never, I think, think of me in this way. I'm sorry, but do I sound to you absurdly silly and pompous over all this?
PIPEMAN: (*puff*).
GIRL: What I should like to do would be to start all over again with him—get back to the mutual interest in work we've always had together. . . .
PIPEMAN: (*bup-bup-bup*).
GIRL: What? Do you see what I mean? Because apart from any question of—well, falling in love really with each other there's always been this—something—between us which is quite outside love—not better or worse but outside it. I can't talk straight, but—do you see—
PIPEMAN: (*the long spittle effect*).

If these effects are rightly timed, the girl will feel not only that she has been talking well, but that she has never been given such sympathetic advice by such an intelligent listener.

without looking at anything or anybody very special, "Do we know that?" quietly but definitely plonkingly. We are grateful to B. Campbell for many of his suggestions here and also for his ready scientific attitudeship when cornered in committee and asked genuine questions about birds. His answer is basically "I don't know," the Socrates ploy: and these replies are probably soundly worded and would, I expect, read like this, e.g.:

Q: *Do robins have spotted eggs?*
A: We shall all of us know more about that when we have a longer series to work on.
or
Well, that's really David Lack's speciality, isn't it, and it's a bit sort of—well, awkward—if I go barging in on his territory. Look, I know Lack . . . etc.,[1]
or
Ask me in nine months' time. We've got a mass of facts—not yet in very good order.
or
You're taking a terrific lot for granted if you use the word "spot," aren't you?

A Test Case.

B. Campbell draws attention to the gambitous nature of the tendency of that very O.K. Birdsman M. Nicholson to call birds by somewhat archaic though of course perfectly authentic names. The wider O.K.-ness is involved in this difficult problem. Is it not fundamentally *correct* scientific attitude play to give the faintest possible pat on the head to the

[1] P. Scott is also decidedly an O.K. birdsman name. Which of the two is actually the robin specialist is not known.

brightest jewels in the diadem of English verbal felicity? Anyhow, that is the Nicholsonian theory. The process, according to Campbell, is known as "throstling" or "dunnocking" ("dunnock" for "hedge-sparrow", "throstle" for *Turdus philomelos clarkei clarkei clarkei*[1]). But long ago during an abortive aeroplane trip I gave it the rank of ploy with the name "smale foulesmanship"—and the name has stuck.

I have said enough, I hope, to show that Birdsmen are natural Lifemen. The kind of question we shall be dealing with in 1953 is Counter-birdsmanship, and it will certainly be one of our headaches. The W.W.W. (Windermere Watcher Watchers) are a small Lakeland society who try to force ornithologists into the one-down position by observing them, taking little notes about them, publishing minute pamphlets about them, writing letters to the *Telegraph* about their first appearance, etc. I believe they have had some slight success. For myself I prefer the Return to Nature Poetry approach, and write J. Fisher[2] letters about fledgling voices in the vocal grove. But looking back over the years, I have to admit that this has been only partially successful.

[1] Experts will note that Lifemanship rejoinder play is to use the Latin name, *but in a slightly out-of-date version*—"for old time's sake."

[2] Another O.K. bird name, though one is bound to admit that Fisher frequently broadcasts, and in programmes which are liked.

XI

TROUTMANSHIP

WHAT A COMPLEX WORLD is here! Yet in the relatively small province of our little Correspondence College we have made enormous headway and gained the thanks of all the fishership community by defining once and for all the two basic trout approaches, in one of which students are expected to satisfy the examiners.

Our Decontamination Reader in Trout, J. Hargreaves, is a pleasant teacher who plays the two-approach system admirably himself. With newcomers, he demonstrates this twoness with a pair of ordinary fishing-rods, one of which is new, the other old.

Rodmanship.

This basic gambit is, basically, the art of being one-up with one's rod. Most commonly, the man who still keeps his old rod is pitted against the man who has just bought a new one. Old Rod makes first move:

OLD ROD (*looking at New Rod's new rod*): I like it. I Like it. I like it. Of course I'm in my forties. I suppose my old one will see me through. Ought to. Ought to. Ought to.

New One (*countering implied criticism*): I was sorry to see my last rod go. . . . But if one really *fishes* in water like this . . . you know . . . I suppose one kills about a rod a season? Mind you, if you don't go in for these acrobatic casts I'm always attempting rather unsuccessfully . . .

Old Rod (*pretending to suspect origin of rod and holding it in his hand*): Tell me—where did you . . . (*our inflection for "where did you" can imply not only that rod was mass produced, but stamped out of synthetic wood.*)

New Rod: Well—you know—"Jackie" Bampton happens to be rather a friend of mine. And my difficulty is that I'm not really comfy unless the action is, well, inches nearer the butt than normal——

Old Rod (*out-gambited but fighting back*): Don't worry . . . don't worry . . . it's like a woman. You get used to it. In a couple of years, anyhow, it will be part of you. Even if you don't catch any trout.

If New Rod's rod is longer, with a longer line, and if the river needs such a rod, Old Rod will be in difficulty. Spandrel's Underthwart can be used here.

Spandrel (*old rodding*): Nice rod, but it isn't alive till you're about fifteen yards out. I like to throw a shorter line myself.

With right inflection, O.R. can suggest that he is an ancient, almost neolithic, virtuoso of the troutstream, a sort of Red Indian, really, belly to the ground, who finds no difficulty in trout work at ten yards.[1]

---

[1] Rodmanship Advanced for 1952. This year has seen New Rod placed in the one down position by Newer Rod Still. This instrument is made of molecularly reconstituted toilet soap. And though it is associated with wrong-clothesmanship (jacket and trousers clean, and matching) and wrong gadgetmanship (fly-boxes made of perspex) the thing works. We are struggling with this embryonic counter:

Troutmanship Basic.

After practice in the two-approach system with rods, students may then start practising troutmanship proper.

This, too, is essentially an A *vs.* B situation. A the purist, the scholar of dry fly, *vs.* B the rough and ready, the ham, the hack.

Tell me frankly, says A the purist, *were you fishing the water or the rise?*

To counter this accusation of just chucking about, the student trained in Old Rodship should have no difficulty. I'm bound to say that Gattling-Fenn was at his best in this situation. Shirt open to the waist and apparently nut-brown to the navel (actually he wore a "Suntan Gypsyvest"), Gattling was able to imply "For Heaven's sake."

"For Heaven's sake," he said, and the gleam of his almost suspiciously white teeth suggested "I'm just a hobo, son—a tramp. My father, and his father before him,[1] were born natural hunters to a man, like every Englishman born a mother's son."

While suggesting every word of this, Gattling was at the same time able actually to say:

"I had him in a corner—and—yes, I'm bound to

NEWER ROD STILL: Yes, it's the first time these fish on the far side of the bend have had a fly decently presented to them.

COUNTERER: Well, I'm bound to admit it makes fishing easier.

N.R.S.: It certainly does.

COUNTERER: I mean, you *could* use a Mills bomb, I suppose.

[1] This would be Gattling-Fenn's grandfather.

say the fly was a bit damp! Spam Special. Yes, I had to rob the sandwich. . . ."

The following Hargreaves Hampers are worth study, and are useful to others besides troutmen.

1. Do not cast in presence of other fishermen. Proved odds are 93 to 1 against anything happening. So if A says: "Have a go at him," you, B, should reply either: "No—you. I had a good day yesterday," *or*: "Oh, that one? He's nearly had me once already. Ruddy great chub."

2. For use against man who catches fish bigger than yours in same water.

TROUTMAN: That's a good one. What does it weigh?
LAYMAN (*cool*): I don't carry scales.
TROUTMAN: I'll weigh it for you . . . 1¾ pounds. That's funny. How long is it?
LAYMAN: Frankly, I don't carry a tape measure either.
TROUTMAN: I do. . . . Thought so. Nearly 16 inches. That's the trouble with this water, it won't stand fish this size. Ought to be two pounds. It's gone back.

Layman begins to realise he has caught a fish almost on its knees and practically fainting for want of food. He could have picked it out of the water with his bare hands.

3. Rub it in. If, for instance, rival makes clumsy cast, go on and on pointing it out. Thus:

TROUTMAN (*smiling through clenched teeth*): *Now* you've put him down. Now you *have* put him down. Crikey, were you trying to brain him? Doubt if he'll put his nose up for a week. Should think he'd rather drown.

I'll move upstream a bit, I think. Happens to all of us.

Marshall's Mangler.

This subject is still very "young" as we call it at Yeovil—i.e. there is still a lot of loose fishing play within our orbit, and a dozen gambits not yet properly described. That is why I am glad to mention Marshall's "Mangler"—a gambit invented by H. Marshall and needing a finesse and urbanity of execution which totally belie its sobriquet.

The general object is to express an enormous Upper Sixthism so devastating that practically no one else can ever speak about fishing again; and it is done in this way.

The catching of your specific fish is *a Problem*, and must be so approached, without fervour, without even enjoyment.

On one side of your equation is your possible fly, *x*: on the other, certain variables.

Let α = weather forecast.

γ = weather.

γ^i = flow of stream in relation to mean number of solid factory deposits and old cans.

β = probable age of trout.

o = probable age of fisherman.

π = distance of nearest active motor-bicycle or farm tractor.

δ = temperature of fish.

Then, by a simple calculation jotted down in a

waterproof tent with unrunnable ink on unsmudg-able paper, Marshall would get some such equation as this:

$$x = \frac{\delta^{16} \circ \sqrt{a^3 \gamma} \quad \gamma^i - 8}{\beta^2 \pi} = \begin{array}{l} \text{Split's Indefatigable } \textit{or} \\ \text{Aunt Mary's Special} \end{array}$$

Hand this result with your rod to the ghillie and walk quite slowly away, leaving him to catch the actual fish. Marshall has learnt to intensify the effect of all this by turning up on the bank in a bowler hat and a dark pin-stripe and a pair of thin, blindingly well-polished, black shoes, in which he delicately picks his way back through pool and undergrowth.

XII

THE ART OF

NOT ROCK-CLIMBING

Rock Play of Odoreida

"Just-a-Scrambleship," as Rockmanship is sometimes nicknamed, is actually taught in the grounds of our College where, between the croquet lawn and the putting-green, is an imitation concrete precipice, four feet high with a three-foot drop to a spring mattress. Believing that demonstration in the field is essential, students are here taught on the spot how

122

to talk about "holds," "grips" and "nice little prob-
lems," and how to come unstuck without actually
mentioning it.

This art has a special interest for students of
Gamesmanship and Lifemanship—not surprising
when it is realised that it is the adopted relaxation
of G. Odoreida. Some of Odoreida's gambits are
objected to by the older members of our Council, but
if Odoreida is the name on every rockman's lips, no
less is he referred to as chief authority, by ourselves,
in that aspect of this art which may be sub-titled:
"How to climb rocks without actually going up
them."

Our Matterhorn[1] Readers, K. Fitzgerald and B.
Hilton-Jones, have described in a definitive conversation the technique of Odoreidaism, and from their
comments this analysis is borrowed freely.

Students of Gameslife will be aware that in the
actual playing of games Odoreida, though often
seen on the edge of a cricket field, was a complete
rabbit. The weight in his pear-shaped figure,
although suggesting the attitude of one accustomed
to standing at fairly deep mid-off, was so unusually
distributed that genuine climbing looked to be, and
was, almost impossible. Besides, it is known that on
heights he once said he was "frightened he might
throw himself over."

It was therefore plucky of Odoreida to life his way
into this reputation of his as a skilled rockclimber.

[1] The original name remains, although the Matterhorn is no longer
an O.K. mountain.

How did he do it?

Odoreida Rock Basic is to be the Man Looking On. Older now, he is inclined, he tells us amusedly, for slippers. In that little place at Pen-y-gwryd, he is never very far from the fire.

There he will be knowledgeable about past climbs, or present routes. "Yes," he says. Odoreida is encouraging at first. "I do consider the bottom pitch of Charity to be harder than anything on Cloggy." He speculates. "You know" (making the wet sucking noise on pipe (see p. 113)), "I've always thought the wall on Craig Yr Ysfa would go."

At this point an absolute stranger or complete new boy might begin to call Odoreida "sir."

"Would you, sir?"

"Well, one or two of us saw it the other day on a top rope. I think it would go. By the way, I see you are still using those nails."

New Boy is made to feel the nails in his boots are unsafe, or out of date. Having by this and that prepared a Lifeman's wicket, Odoreida goes in to bat. Essentially his is climb avoidance play, while seeming to be eager. I know all Yeovil men will want to join me in emphasising the importance of this gambit.

The H'm Tinge

Maybe he's not going to climb just now because it's the wrong time of year. In June, Odoreida says, "I only like Great Gully at Christmas-time when it's full of ice." At Christmas, on the other hand, he recalls that everyone's done it every Christmas, and that everyone is doing it now. In fact it's pretty well got Stop-and-Go lighting.

Somebody else says something else is a difficult climb.

"Well—I seem to remember when Jack did it he did 'Sunset' afterwards. After all, the Caldecott brothers took 140 pounds of photographic equipment along that ledge in 1903."

A "h'm" climate is built up.

"The Sceptre presents the same problem—only I suppose ten times more tricky. But I was rather surprised to find ironmongery all over the cliff—the whole place is getting bunged up with it. Bad as the Matterhorn. Look, I found this halfway up Great Slab the other day. Look."

I knew that Odoreida always keeps a rusty piton, scarcely an O.K. climbing aid in this district, always in his pocket, and that he casts doubt on actual climbers by "finding" it. Occasionally he has a rather technical way of saying a boot climb ought to be done in rubbers (or vice versa). Thus:

"No, I don't think so."

So few climbs seem worth while to Mr. Odoreida, thinks New Boy.

"No—I should have to take my rubbers. And it's essentially a boot climb. But the holds are so worn now. But you go, if you want a nice scamper in a pair of gym shoes. I've got my *War and Peace*."

"Good old Wagger-Pagger," replied Gattling-Fenn once, knowing that Odoreida had never read this book, though he was always being found with it in chimney corners.[1]

If really pressed, Odoreida would be quite frank about it. "No," he would say.

"Frankly I'm frightened of it."

LAYMAN: Don't blame you. Hardly any holds of any kind, are there?

O: Well, the holds which do arrive, arrive well. Not holds perhaps—certain helpful rugosities. . . . But . . . no, I've got my family, and I think if one's got a family . . .[2] No. For me Pinnacle Wall is out of bounds.

The danger of Odoreidaism was shown when he sometimes almost convinced *himself* that he was or had been an expert climber, and began talking himself dangerously near to having to make a climb himself. But he could always take refuge in the "frankly I'm getting older" defence.

"The trouble is," he might say, after dinner, "I get so tired standing on one leg looking for the next hold. Coming down I wanted to smoke—but I was finger-jamming all the way. . . ."

The New Boy may move in closer, now, to listen. "Only the crook of a finger between Odoreida and eternity," he thinks to himself.

Feeling himself in form, Odoreida might now develop the Other Interest move.

[1] Odoreida's only genuine reading, besides the *Rockclimbers' Record*, which he memorised for its technical terms, was *Whitaker's Almanack*, in which he liked to check up on the salaries of his many acquaintances in the Civil Service.

[2] The only person this could possibly refer to is Odoreida's sister-in-law, bolster-thighed Paulette Odoreida, whom he only saw once a year when he took the Odoreida children to the annual opening of the Chelmsford roller-skating rink.

"No. This was in '36. I thought an off-day was about due . . . and I heard that that lovely little Alpine ranunculus mentioned in Butcher—a kingcup in miniature—had been seen on the Devil's Cliff in 1876 . . . and of course I knew that Hanging Garden Gully has been stripped to the bone by botanists, from the local High School I guess . . . so I thought I'd have a look at the Kitchen proper . . . and there it was, well, just inside the mouth. I think I shall always remember it. Seeing that flower."

I heard this and of course was simply waiting for the laugh. Odoreida and spring flowers!

"How did you get *there*, Odoreida?" I said.

Somebody said "Sh!" Odoreida turned smiling towards me.

"Oh, I went up the first couple of pitches of Advocate's Wall, then broke out to the Gut for about thirty feet . . ."

SELF: That's new surely? . . .

O: Well as a matter of fact I think it probably is. . . . Having to finish up the wall was too sticky altogether for what I call good climbing.

NEW BOY: But that's one for the log, isn't it?

O: My days for logging climbs are over—that's for you younger people. But I'm afraid it is known, now, isn't it, as Odoreida's Rib? Of course, I wanted it called after Messinger, because he first saw it. And it was only chance that I found myself on it at all. The whole thing reminds me of the day I nearly got stuck in Lockwood's chimney.

I couldn't help joining, though for different reasons, in the respectful smiles which followed this, and

made no use of my private knowledge that years ago
Odoreida, lost in the mist when going to post a
letter, really did get stuck near the foot of this climb,
and insisted on being pulled out by three lady members of the Pinnacle Club and a Brownie.

XIII

CLUBMANSHIP

THAT SO TYPICAL institution of this island, the Club, has aptly been described as the normal field of exercise, if not the happy hunting-ground, of the astute Lifeman. Knowledge of some Club play therefore is considered an essential qualification for Lifemastership.

I propose in this chapter first briefly to outline Club Basic and then to analyse only one, but a very important one, of the main gambits which are essentially Club and which *for that reason* (and because the particular is the only true general) have the wide application always implied in the local.[1]

1. CLUB BASIC

The Two Club Approach.

Clubmanship proper consists, I always believe, in the continuous implication that you have Another Life, so that even if you dig into your club regularly at 11.45 a.m. every day and stay there till, dazed with smoke, you feel your way out at midnight, you can still give the impression that it is a question of dropping in for a moment's rest, quiet drink or chat

[1] The local referred to in this paragraph is, of course, the Black Lion, Hammersmith.

in between violent spasms of key jobs or valuable social activity.

Certain coarse and obvious ways of trying to show your important independence we have denounced as Sloppy Lifemanship. It is quite wrong to bustle into the Club and tell the Hall Porter that if any messages come through you're "not in." The porter will know and may even say that there have been no messages, not even a postcard, for eight weeks. Unsubtle and vulnerable, this approach is termed by us *Lifecorny*.

Never make the mistake, either, of not remembering who your fellow clubmen are. On the contrary, know the names and, if possible, the salaries, of everybody, especially if they don't know who you are. Take an interest in their professions. Be actually extremely nice to any crotchety club servant there happens to be and to unusually old members, particularly if they are expiring. It is by such little gracious acts, combined with enquiries about "that nephew of yours with chronic nosebleed" that one-upness is established. Then you can pounce.

Basic Club Play as we teach it is the Two Club Approach. In other words, it is essential to belong to two clubs if you belong to one club. It doesn't matter if your second club is a 5/- a-year sub. affair in Greek Street: the double membership enables you, when at your main or proper club, to speak often in terms of regretful discrimination about the advantages of your Other One.

But for those who play the genuine Two Club

Forcing Approach, both clubs should be roughly of equal standing, and, if possible, O.K. Then, if the two clubs are of sufficiently contrasted character, which they must be, a fascinating set of ploys can be brought into operation. The essence of the technique, of course, is to maintain the condition of being, as F. H. Bradley, genial old Mertonian, once wrote in a different context—"the other in the other."

I.e. supposing your two clubs are called, to use a thin disguise, the Artillery and the Studio Arts, basic play is to appear in the artistic club very much a member of the military. Exhibit quite a light touch, in the modern military manner, at the Studio, but maintain a basically clipped appearance, hair short-looking, with bowler hat and the correct clothes for the Eastern fringe of W.1. Ask somebody to "explain" the work of H. Moore, and listen quietly attentive as if knowing perhaps a bit more than you let on, but remain definitely incisive and a well-disciplined clubman, silent in the silent room, snookering quietly in the snooker-room, drinking soberly at the bar.

When, however, at the Artillery, be quite different, in fact the opposite. Be enervated from your pottery designing at Chiswick, in huge red corduroys and an indigo shirt. Early on, perhaps, you have pointed yourself out by presenting a picture, a particularly abstract abstract, Paris 1926, to the committee. Already it hangs, if in a very dark corner, near the Lucy Kemp-Welch picture of the Omdurman charge. In mien you are, perhaps, suffering, in

FIG. 31. THE TWO CLUB FORCING APPROACH (1).

Hugo Coating at the Studio Arts dressed as a member of the Artillery.

accordance with the view which you think Artillery holds of the way the artist behaves. You are certainly abstract. Walking into the library, a man who has specialised in this work, Hugo Coating, suddenly holds his hand over his eyes and says, "Oh, my God." When he said it again at the other end of the library a Lieut.-General Broax once said, "What are you 'My Godding' about?"

"I think perhaps . . ." began a more sensitive member—a young Captain in the Light Ack Ack.

"I'm sorry, but I praised something I thought was bad. Something that I knew really was bad. Oh, God."

"Oh yes," said Broax.

FIG. 32. THE TWO CLUB FORCING APPROACH (2).
The same man (Hugo Coating) at the Artillery dressed as a member of the Studio Arts.

"That is the only untruth."

"How about a cordial?" said Broax, with a look of rough sympathy, seeing that Coating had flung himself face downwards on the settee and kept knocking the arm of it with the instep of his upturned foot. And Coating was often being timidly offered drinks in this way, and though he seldom offered the other half, before long he was able to do what he liked in the Artillery and was a sort of authority, and it was taken for granted that it was perfectly O.K. for Coating to sit in the seat with arms at the head of the long table. Coating became as respected at the Artillery for his Studio Arts background as he was at the Arts for his "in the services" tone.

2. A Gambit Analysed

The Affair at the Monosyllable.

Queer aspects of Clubmanship, extraordinary instances, are often brought to our notice by students, and their treatment becomes part of our regular teaching. No harm, now, in revealing that G. Odoreida, with his revolutionary but often coarsely effective Lifemanship of the Left, has a brother, V. Odoreida (husband of rocking-horse-nostrilled Paulette Odoreida) who, it is now well known, is still farther to the Left than his brother G. Heaven knows we do not recommend the ploys and gambits of this man for the use of genuine Lifemen, but there is no sense in denying that they exist.

"The Monosyllable" is not the real name of a club. It stands nevertheless for one of the genuinely exclusive clubs the names of all of which, Lifemen will have observed, are, lifishly enough, only one syllable long. Only Cogg-Willoughby, of our staff, has succeeded in making the membership of one of these. G. Odoreida, of course, scoffed and V., his brother, was almost maddened by Cogg's success. He determined on a counter. An incident occurred which we may as well outline. As the members of the Monosyllable were trickling one by one towards the dining-room, a message came for Cogg.

"Your guest has arrived, sir."

Cogg stopped in midstream to look round. Had he forgotten? Who? A voice came.

"Hallo, Len, I'm sorry I'm late."

Cogg turned like a shot at this hated abbreviation of a Christian name he had always tried to suppress. A dozen members must have turned with him to see V. Odoreida standing with a long coil of ticker tape paper held before steel-rimmed spectacles and wearing a shirt slightly soiled and *open at the neck, no tie.*

Cogg had just enough presence of mind left to blurt out "Thank you. And could you clean the plugs as well?" But he felt few were deceived. He rushed from the scene, leaving by some servants' exit. But the damage to Cogg's confidence was lasting. It was at least three months before he next visited the Monosyllable.

XIV

WINESMANSHIP

Definitions.

WINESMANSHIP WAS ONCE listed as a department of
Clubmanship. But although it is itself only a province, albeit a vast one, of the area roughly defined
as the Gracious Living Gambit of Lifemanship,
Winesmanship may play a big part, sooner or later,
in the lives of all of us.

A schoolboy definition of Winesmanship is "How
to talk about wine without knowing a Hock from a
Horse's Neck." But in fact Winesmanship is itself a
philosophy if not an ethic, and can be used in Young
Manship, in Jobmanship, even in wooing.

Winesmanship Basic.

A few phrases and a ploy or two, to get our bear-
ings. Consider the simplest approach first. If you
are taking a girl, or even a former headmaster, out
to lunch at a restaurant, it is WRONG to do what
everybody else does—namely, to hold the wine list
just out of sight, look for the second cheapest claret
on the list, and say, "Number 22, please." Never
say the number, anyhow, because it suggests that
you are unable to pronounce the name of the wine
you are ordering. Nominate the wine in English

French, and make at the same time some comment which shows at least that you have heard of it before. Say, for instance:

"They vary, of course, but you seldom get a complete dud."

Or simply:

"I wonder . . ."

A useful thing is to look at the wine list before the waiter comes and say, "Amazing. Nothing here you can be sure of. Yet the food is quite good. But I've got an idea."

Then, when the waiter comes, say to him, "Look. You've got a Château Neon '45 somewhere secreted about the place, I know. Can you let us have a bottle?"

(You know he's got it because you have in fact read it off the wine list, cheapest but one.)

When the waiter leaves, you can say, "They keep a small cache for favoured customers."

With a little trouble a really impressive effect, suitable for average city-man guest, can be made by arriving fifteen minutes early, choosing some cheap ordinaire, and getting waiter to warm and decant it. When guest comes, say, "I know you'll like this. Should be all right. I got them to get it going at nine o'clock this morning. Not expensive but a perfectly honest wine—and a *good* wine if it's allowed to breathe for three or four hours."

For Home Winesmanship, remember that your mainstay is hypnotic suggestion. Suggest that some rubbishy sherry, nine bob, is your special pride, and

FIG. 33. WINESMANSHIP: A LITTLE-KNOWN PLOY.

After saying (not of course really having a cellar) "I'll get it from the cellar," enter any cupboard (preferably beneath stairs), *close door*, and make sound with feet as if descending to and (after pause) mounting from a wine-cellar.

has a tremendously individual taste. Insist on getting it yourself "from the cellar." Take about four minutes uncorking it. Say, "I think decanting destroys it," if you have forgotten, or are too bored, to decant it. Keep staring at the bottle before you pour it. When you have drawn the cork, look particularly hard at the cork, and, of course, smell it.

For the first sip of the wine, here are some comments for Student Winesmen. Remember, if the wine is claret, 1920 St. Emilion Château Cheval Blanc, that strangely enough absolutely everybody is supposed to know whether it is a claret or a burgundy. Remember also that practically absolutely everybody is supposed to recognise instantly the year. Practically almost absolutely everybody should be able to say "St. Emilion." The only tiny shade of doubt which can enter your comment is about its being Château Cheval Blanc.

Don't say too much about the wine being "sound" or "pleasant": people will think you have simply been mugging up a wine-merchant's catalogue. It is a little better to talk in broken sentences and say, "It has . . . don't you think?" Or, "It's a little bit cornery," or something equally random like "Too many tramlines." I use this last phrase because it passes the test of the *boldly meaningless*.

An essential point to remember is that everybody is supposed to take it for granted that every wine has its *optimum year* up to which it progresses, and beyond which it falls about all over the place. E.g. you can give interest to your bottle of four-and-sixpenny British Russet by telling your guest that you "wish he had been able to drink it with you when it was at the top of its form in forty-nine."

Alternatively you can say, "I'm beginning to like this. I believe it's just on the brink." Or I rather like saying, "I drink this now for sentimental reasons only . . . just a pleasant residue, an essence of sugar and water—but still with a hint of former glories. Keep it in your mouth for a minute or two . . . see what I mean?" Under this treatment, the definitive flavour of carbolic which has been surprising your guest will seem to him to acquire an interest if not a grace.

Alternatively you may admit, frankly, that your four-and-sixpenny is a failure. "They were right," you say. "The twenty-fours should have been won-derful. Perfect grapes, perfect weather, and the *vestre*—the Dordogne wind. But for some reason or other they mostly sulked. Taste it and tell me what you think. You may like it."

Or if your four-and-sixpenny is only two years old and unbearably acid, you can say, "Let it rest in your mouth. Now swallow. There! Do you get it? That 'squeeze of the lemon,' as it's called . . ."

Then, if there is no hope of persuading Guest that what he is drinking has any merit whatever, you can talk of your bottle as an Academic Interest treat.

"Superb wine, but it has its periods of recession. Like a foot which goes to sleep, has pins and needles, and then recovers. I think that was André's[1] expla-nation. At the moment it's BANG in the middle of one of its WORST OFF-COLOUR PERIODS."

Watch your friend drink this wine, and if he shudders after it, and makes what we winesmen call "the medicine face," you can say . . . "Yes! You've got it? Let it linger a moment."

"Why?" says Guest.

"Do you notice the after-sharpness, the point of asperity in the farewell, the hint of malevolence, even, in the *au revoir*?" If he says, "Yes," as he will, look pleased.

Note on Tastingship.

Many Yeovil Lifemen are so completely ignorant of wine of all kinds that in our small pamphlet AC/81

[1] André Simon, completely O.K. wine name.

we have had to tell them that the red wines are red in colour and, confusing point, the white yellow. It may not be out of place if I remind general readers here, too, that *method of drinking* is an essential accompaniment to *method of comment*.

Before drinking, or rather sipping, the wine, you smell it for bouquet. *Not* with a noisy sniff but *silently and delicately*, perhaps making a funnel of your hands to concentrate the essence. G. Gibbs used to create some effect by smelling the stem of the glass as well, but there is no real point in this. A good general rule is to state that the bouquet is better than the taste, and vice versa.

In sipping, do not merely sip. Take a mouthful and chew it, making as much noise as you can. Having thus attracted attention, you can perform some of the evolutions favoured by that grand old Winesman Bath-Meriton. The most ordinary method he used was to lean his head forward so that his rather protruberant ears were extended like the wings of a monoplane and drink the wine from the far side of his glass. To get the bouquet he would smell it first with the left nostril, closing the other with his forefinger, and then with the right. He would also hold it up to the light and then shine a small pocket torch

FIG. 34. THE BATH-MERITON
POSITION FOR DRINKING FROM
FAR SIDE OF GLASS.

containing what really looked like a miniature fog lamp through from the other side! He would dip the end of his handkerchief in the wine and then hold the dipped end up to the light. And remember, when it actually comes to the tasting, sip from the *far* side of the glass. Gattling-Fenn once said, "Why not simply turn the glass the other way round?"

Winesmanship Advanced.

The average guest, who knows no more about wine than the Winesman himself, can be easily impressed by such methods. But there are men who genuinely know something of this subject, and they are a very different problem.

I used to advise a simple and direct approach with such people, including an anglicising of the simplest French words (e.g. call the Haut Brion the High Bryon). Gattling-Fenn at his first Saintsbury Club dinner realised that it was 1,000 to 1 the man on his left knew more about wine than he did. So he said (of an old burgundy, using the recommended Ordinary Approach):

"Like it?"

EXPERT: Yes.
GATTLING: It's good.
EXPERT: Yes, but you know what's happened?
GATTLING: Yes—in a way. What?
EXPERT: It's been poured through the same strainer that they used for the Madeira.

Gattling broke into a hearty laugh at this, which quickly froze as he realised from the puzzled faces round him that the expert was speaking seriously.

No—the only method with the true specialist is what we call Humble Studentship, mixed in with perhaps *two* carefully memorised genuine advanced facts.

There are, however, lesser specialists, semi-amateurs, perhaps trying a little amateur winesmanship on their own, for whom we recommend the following advanced methods.

1. *Beaded-bubbleship.* This obscurely-titled ploy is merely the art of speaking, and especially writing, about wine as if it was one of the O.K. Literary Things. Be vague by being literary. Talk of the "imperial decay" of your invalid port. "Its gracious withdrawal from perfection, keeping a hint of former majesty withal, as it hovers between oblivion and the divine *Untergang* of infinite recession."

Smiling references to invented female literary characters are allowed here. "The sort of wine Miss Mitford's Emily would have offered Parson Square, sitting in the window-seat behind the chintz curtains."

2. *Percentageship* is, of course, the opposite method, and designed to throw a different kind of haze, the figure fog, over the wine conversation. Remarks like "The consumption of 'treated' vermouth rose from 47.5 in 1924 to 58.9 in 1926 . . ." will impart a considerable degree of paralysis to any wine conversation. So will long lists of prices, or imaginary percentages of glucosity in contrasted champagnes, or remarks about the progress in the quality of cork trees, or the life-cycle of *Vinoferous demoliens*,

little-known parasite now causing panic in the Haut-Baste.

It is always possible, if a wine completely stumps you, to talk in general terms about winemanly subjects.

If it is a warm summer day, say that "dear old Cunoisier will be getting worried about the fermentation of his musts."[1]

But if in real difficulties, remember that there are moments when the pickaxe is a more useful instrument than the most delicate surgeon's forceps. And I shall always remember Odoreida thrusting aside sixteen founder members of the Wine and Food Society with a "Well, let's have a real drink," and throwing together a mixture which left them breathless.

"Pop-skull, they called it in Nevada,"[2] he said,

[1] If you have reason to think that your guest is not particularly up in American madeiras, quote the following words in a plonking voice: "There was an 1842 which Sohier took the trouble to bring all the way to London from Boston and gave us in 1938 (11th April) at the Ritz; the voyage had upset it and it had not had time to recover from the shock."

[2] A basic subdivision of Winesmanship is the U.S. hard-drink gambit and the question of its counters. The U.S. gambit is to be amused when anybody orders sherry, and to flock round and watch it being drunk, particularly in a club at six o'clock. It is an exaggeration to say that they expect the drinker to bring out knitting or start reading *Old Mother Goose*, but they are interested.

Nevertheless, the deliberate drinking of sherry will wear many U.S. men down, particularly, of course, if it is mixed with a rather pi-faced lecture on the American "inability to enjoy wine" and a richly exaggerated account of one's own national habits with drink, making your audience really believe that every typical British family serves a different wine at a different temperature with every course.

A wholly different counter to the U.S. icy hard-drink gambit, based on our management of religious men, is to go one better. Serve drinks yourself so cold that they are frozen to the glass and have to and poured two parts of vodka into one of sherry and three of rum, adding a slice cut from the disc of a sunflower.

---

be filed out and chewed. Let your Martinis be mixed in a much stronger proportion of gin to vermouth than six to one, in fact, some counter-U.S. experts pour vermouth into the glass and then pour it out again, lightly mopping the sides with their handkerchiefs, and then fill the glass with what is, of course, neat gin. Another ploy is to invent some "little drink" or name of a drink which "everybody is drinking in Nevada" (all Americans admire the suggestion that you have been to Nevada). Call it not "Frozen Larynx" or "Surgeon's Knife," which is 1937-38, but Martini, mixing two absolute disparates as in the Odoreida Iceberg described above. Then peck at it and say, "Oh for a real Martini—a big Martini, one you can pull over your head like a jersey" (phrase of U.S. Lifeman 46, reported to me in April 1952 by U.S.1).

XV

CHRISTMAS GIFTMANSHIP

A VISITOR TO OUR College may be agreeably surprised to find a tiny room devoted to Present Giving and Good Cheer. Surprised, I say, because sometimes we are given the reputation of being spoilsports at Yeovil, or told that our Science is a dour one.

Not a bit of it. We have many laughs in and out of hours: and good nature and geniality, at the right season, are encouraged to reign—encouraged, of course, so long as the Lifeman retains his prior right of one-upness.

All of us think of Christmas, particularly, as a time when the spirit of friendliness, of being unusually nice to children especially, should prevail. Yet the alert Lifeman, even at this time of the year, apparently so unfavourable to basic gambiting, knows that he can make the recipient of his niceness feel unpleasant, if slightly.

It was Gattling-Fenn, good Lifeman and great Christmas expert, known for his Favourite Uncle play (see *Lifemanship*, p. 112) who first described the "Remember Mrs. Wilson" gambit (see the special edition of *Lifemanship* printed for the Vassar Foundation). Gattling, by exploding comic sausages, would rouse the children to a pitch of frenzy and then suddenly tell them not to make too much noise because of Mrs. Wilson, a mythical invalid.

It was only last year, however, that I realised the delicacy of Gattling's actual technique with the actual giving of presents.

If I may summarise Gattling-Fenn, the object of Christmas Giftmanship is:

1. To make it seem to everybody present that the receiver is getting something better than he has given you.

2. To make the receiver feel that you have got away with a present that looks all right but which he knows isn't really.

3. To make the receiver feel there is some implied criticism about the present you have chosen.

To take the last section first because it is the simplest and the easiest to explain: a rather dowdy-looking and badly made-up woman who prides herself on "not always dabbing herself with a powder-puff" can in certain tones of voice effectively be given the present of a beauty box. Conversely, a woman who is insidiously ostentatious about the flower-like and impersonal quality of her beauty can be given a hot-water bottle, a small biscuit-coloured Shetland shawl to wear in bed, or a tin of patent food which announces clearly on the front label that it has been specially treated to be made more easily digestible. Add a shopping bag (a group of friends may arrange together to give this lot as a set) and the effect is almost bound to be annoying over a long period and especially in retrospect. Particularly if, thrown in with the rest, somebody can give her one cheap lipstick smelling of lard.

Under this same head come special presents to men who fancy themselves remarkably young for their age. A spectacle case, for instance, for the man unwilling to disclose the fact that he wears glasses: or, best of all, a small "YOU AND ME" sound amplifier "which anybody over the age of 25 is bound to find useful when listening to conversation in a noisy crowded room."[1]

For the going-one-better ploy, one must act quickly

---

[1] A good deal of work has been done on the dialogue for this particular item. This was demonstrated in the Fourth Lifemanship Lecture ("Sloppy Yuleship"). Here is the actual dialogue or parlette:

LIFEMAN (*handing small strangely shaped parcel*): Happy Christmas.
LAY RECEIVER: What?
L.: I said "Happy Christmas." Something for you.
L.R.: Oh, I say. . . . (*Paper unwrapping*) What on earth ? . . .
L.: Like it?
L.R.: Yes. What is it?
L.: Try it. No . . . look . . . put this little thing in your ear. It's a sound amplifier.
L.R.: What for?
L.: It amplifies sound. When it's difficult to listen—in a crowded room—put it in your ear and wear the battery in your buttonhole—do you see? Let me . . . it's not a real carnation, it's only a dummy —and if you have the least difficulty in hearing——
L.R.: But I'm not——
L.: No, of course you're not. Of course you're not. Of course you're not. But—anyone over the age of 25, really, finds it difficult to hear in a crowded room. It's not that you're deaf. Here. Let me talk to you through it. (*Then recite some poem very loudly but with mouth well to side of microphone of machine*)
   There was a boy, ye knew him once,
   Ye cliffs and islands of Winander——
L.R.: Of what?
L.: WINANDER. Wonderful, isn't it?
L.R.: Thanks very much.

and buy the present for the giver immediately one has received the gift. If a man gives you (if you are a woman) a handbag, you should give him a cigarette case *with initials on it* to hint that you have taken more care and he must do better next time. If somebody gives you one of those *de luxe* editions of Jane Austen in a stand-up cardboard case, you can immediately buy any old nineteenth-century copy of a George Eliot novel and make the Jane Austen giver feel he is merely a trier by telling him you have hunted four years for this example "of the Bristol edition" (you can call it a "Bristol first"), and that when you found it six months ago you knew he would be the person to appreciate it. At the same time, Jane Austen will half realise he is being fooled and that you have probably only paid half a dollar for it, anyhow.

In more advanced work, poor relations may be maddened by giving them useful presents, like scissors or bradawls. Eminent art critics can be given the World's Best Twenty Masterpieces in Oil, done in rather poor colour reproduction, with the dirty pinks merely brown and the browns merely dirty.

A jolly little poker-work doggie which pops in and out of a kennel shaped like a shoe is a splendid present to give to either (*a*) a zoologist, (*b*) a collector of Staffordshire glaze, or (*c*) a breeder of pedigree poodles. To one's wife, of course, one gives the present one wants oneself—a book on astronomy, for instance, or even one on golf, "in the hope that she will really start to play, now."

A keen gardener, who knows something about gardening, can be enormously irritated by being given a poetry anthology on the theme of garden flowers referring to flowers in the vaguest possible terms and quite often describing spring flowers and autumn flowers coming out at the same time, and vice versa. Golfers who pride themselves on the manly professionalism of their equipment can be given golf mittens embroidered with knitted nose-gays.

It is rather a good thing to give expensive presents (*a*) to people who think they are helping you financially, or better still (*b*) to those to whom you owe money.

Any man who prides himself on the period accuracy of his room decoration can be given a crinoline lady to fit over a telephone ("Grenfell's Good Turn").

If a hired servant, give your employer something better than he has given you. If you receive an obviously dud present, such as a cheap china sweet tray, when the giver next comes to the house to dine place her present ostentatiously in the middle, with your own sweet trays (silver, and of obviously better design) grouped round it.

If the boss, it is a good thing to give to your employees a calendar consisting of an owl with little numbers under it which have to be moved every day. They will have to be moved every day.

Wonders can be done with a genuinely old painted tray, one handle of which, however, has been broken off so many times that it consists entirely of glue and falls to the ground after half an hour by its own weight. After handle has come off twice, you can say fairly sharply to recipient: "Yes, I'm afraid it was born in an age when mass-production was unknown."

But Gattling is at his Christmas-ship best when it comes to the treatment of children. His basic gambit is to give them presents a couple of years below their age-group. If the child is continuously burying itself in a corner with *Lord Jim*, give it a book about a wild wolf dog which saves a baby from an eagle. If the boy is in the space-travel, space-ship phase, give him any book in which animals talk and hedgehogs wear a watch and chain. Or to any child over seven, just getting really interested in revolvers and sawn-off shotguns, Gattling may, with that genial twinkle, give a book printed on indestructible paper with special "Childprufe" binding about Duckie the Cock and his adventures in Woollie-Woolla Land.

FIG. 35. LIFEMANSHIP ACCESSORIES LIMITED

F. Wilson has improvised this dummy "Petit Chalet" cuckoo clock, with extra-loud cuckoo at quarters, and dustpan-and-brush-proof packing shavings with special ADHERO barb ensuring that each has to be removed from the carpet by manual torsion.

(Note ring on little finger of hand on left supplied by our Department of Foreign Amity with a small point on the inward side, for slightly pricking the grasped hand.)

XVI

HANDS-ACROSS-THE-SEAMANSHIP

IT WAS ONCE said of Yeovil, I think not unjustly, that "the subject of Foreign Relations is neglected here." Now each candidate is expected to show some proficiency in what, reduced to its simplest elements, may be represented as $k\lambda\ 3\cdot26084$, if "k" is the factor of constant international difference[1] and "λ" the vague desire to be pleasant.

It is not our policy continuously to try to be one-up, as a nation, on other nations; but it is our aim to rub in the fact that we are not trying to do this, otherwise what is the point of not trying to do this?

First lessons concentrate on the necessity of always

[1] i.e. the tendency to be faintly irritated by foreigners.

using the same phrases, and using them again and again. No harm in the general reader memorising one or two of them now:

We have a lot in common.
After all, we come from the same stock.
We have a lot to learn from each other.

Plasterman's Approach.

The important thing of course is, when speaking to this man from overseas, to get in first. No one followed this rule more keenly than Gattling-Fenn's half-brother, who was not called Gattling-Fenn at all but Joe Plasterman—whence the whole gambit-sequence involving the use of those phrases sometimes called "Plasterman's Approach."

It is known that once, when Plasterman was a guest at the Monosyllable, he saw two members standing at the bar. He was unknown to these members, *and they were at this time unknown to each other.* But Plasterman's host had happened to mention that one of them was an American.

Plasterman went up to these two men and placed his hands gently on their upper arms, standing between them. Quietly he said:

"The future happiness of the world is based on the friendship of the two peoples."

Then, with a slight downward pressure of his hands on the shoulders of the two, he added: "I won't say any more."

"Do you know those two?" said his host, when Plasterman got back.

"Why not? They are my brothers, aren't they?" said Plasterman, still in the Approach position, but he noticed that his host looked as if he was trying to disappear into himself. Host began to whisper:

"But I mean that was Ed Murrow and Harold Nicolson. They can't both be your brothers. Besides——"

"However unworthy the sower of the seed . . ." began Plasterman; but his host was beginning to edge off, and Plasterman—fate of the Lifeman—was left alone with his one-upness.

Plasterman's work was quickly recognised, and it was not long before he was given a position of trust in the Goodwill Department of the Ministry. It was through Plasterman, actually, that a specifically U.S. Problem came my way, no doubt because I know the States well myself, having lived there for close on thirty days. It was therefore as Founder of the American branch of Games-Life (Principal, J. Bryan III, of Wa.), in conjunction with the Office of American Enthusiasm, that it became my pleasant duty to greet American visitors to Britain in the Festival Year, and appear to be trying to make them feel at home while at the same time becoming one-up on them (G.B.-manship). My pamphlet on the subject has long been delivered to the department concerned and may be printed early in 1965.[1] Here, meanwhile, is the work of our collateral branch on U.S.-manship.

[1] My summary will be published in 1953, Series IV, *Games-Life*.

U.S.-MANSHIP

A note on how, when visiting Britain, to appear to be quite happy to be one-down, while actually remaining one-up.

General Rules.

The basic gambit for all Lifemen, of course, is to praise. And the basic, because slightly annoying, thing for U.S.-men to praise in Britain is its charm. This is sometimes called "Cliffs of Dovership." It can be done with most effect if you praise, and with politeness, the charm or quaintness of any of the following:

(*a*) Pseudo-Tudor, such as the thatched telephone kiosk on the London-Oxford road, or some frightful old barn which has been casting a shadow over your host's garden for years, shortening the lawn-tennis court by two feet, yet incapable of being pulled down, removed or destroyed for lack of money, labour and the necessary pulling-down local government licence.

(*b*) Some bits of condemned and muddy farmland with neglected coppice and untended rivulet, which local residents are particularly ashamed of.

(*c*) Something which the British don't think charming at all but on the contrary particularly up to date and mechanised and modern. Stand, for instance, in front of the new London University building, one of the highest in London, and "love it because it's quaint." Watch one of our most renowned and actually streamlined engines, the Bournemouth Belle or the Coronation Scot, sliding out of its terminus, and say, "I've always

wanted to see a steam-engine again. Why, I remember when the Twentieth Century Limited used
steam." Or ask to be taken on a tour of the largest
British film studios, at Denham, and say, "Why,
it's got everything, cameras, lights, and here's a
little carpenter's shop too."

Another good general ploy when in Britain is to take
for granted absolute ignorance of anything American,
and then be surprised, if not offended, if your
British listener has not heard of some name of purely
local interest. E.g. say, "We have a magazine
called the *New Yorker*" or "There were two President
Roosevelts, you know." *Then* talk without any
explanation but with a wealth of local detail about
"Lausche in the days when he was Mayor of Cleve-
land," and take it for granted that your British listener
will not only be interested but informed.

There is a decidedly irritating way of "being
amused," very difficult to acquire, yet recommended
to the advanced U.S.-man. He will suggest to his
British friend that like all Britons he thinks of American history as beginning with George Washington
and the apple tree, leaping straight to the Boston
Tea Party, jumping thence to Uncle Tom's Cabin
via American Indians being shot down one by one
as they circle round Gary Cooper, and a band of early
settlers who succeeded in preserving America for
Rockefeller and Harpo Marx.

This friendly teasing is irritating because it in-
cludes and subtends a basic gambit, "Grain of
truthship."

Behaviour.

In dress, be either (*a*) keenly American or (*b*) extremely English. But note to Bostonians: extreme Englishness is set off rather than spoilt if one Americanism creeps in: e.g. in day dress it is O.K. not to show cuffs: or (recommended American pronunciation inserted in perfected Bostonian English) retain the American "*mus*-tash" instead of the relatively feeble English "mstarsh."

It is slightly annoying to the English to be told that their English accent is "perfect" or "sweet" or "cute," since the Englishman rightly believes that he alone has no accent whatever. It is also annoying to the English who pride themselves on being able to imitate the American accent to point out that in fact the accent they are trying to reproduce is a mixture of the dialects of six American states, all of which are not less than fifteen degrees south of the Maine accent to which, from its wording and references, the mimicry must belong.

Interest in Cricket.

U.S. visitors must, of course, go to Lord's— sacred-shrine-of-cricket, in an attitude of gentlemanly respect and alert anticipation. If they find while watching the game that for the first twenty minutes absolutely nothing happens, they should not comment on the fact that absolutely nothing happens, but they should suddenly turn to their host and say, "You know, we have heard so much about Lord's in the States. Now I want you to analyse for

me the wonderful atmosphere which they say per-
vades this place." After forty minutes, if a batsman
scores one run, it is coarse U.S.-manship to say,
"Would Di Mag have powdered that one!" Just
say, "Wow."

Make some reference, suggesting that an effort is
being made, to W. G. Grace, England's greatest
genius of cricket, but get one initial wrong, perhaps
the second.

Individual Ploys.

When going to a British Railway station, do not
say anything about the relative miseries of these
spots, but bring galoshes, blankets, air cushion,
packet of sandwiches and own coffee in a thermos.
It is quite a good ploy in England to be seen constantly carrying about coffee in a Thermos.

Conversely, yet perhaps connected with this, it is
rather a good thing, having arrived in Britain by air,
to ignore Westminster Abbey, Parliament Square
and the Tower of London when your host mumbles
something about these places with vague pride, and
say instead, "I can't wait to get to see Waterloo
Station."

Carry with you any example of a recent British
article criticising America, broadmindedly and
genially agree with it, and praise the British for having given such a good example to the Americans of
what the Americans ought to have done. E.g. take
a recent British *Architectural Review* attack on domestic architecture in the United States and read it out

aloud to your British friend while standing amidst the housing accretions of any suburb of any large British town or in any recently built village, and say, "Yes, you certainly have got a way with your domestic architecture which we can't touch over there."

It is quite a good thing to read up bits of local history and literary association, then ask your British friend and guide questions about them. Henry VII's Chapel in Westminster Abbey makes a good background for such knowledgeable questions; or Dove Cottage, home of Wordsworth in the Lakes, with special reference to Coleridge's visits there. In both cases, of course, your British host will be unable to conceal his almost complete ignorance of the facts involved.

If your British friends fail to be put off or made to feel slightly awkward by these delicate little gambits, and mutual friendliness and goodwill insist on breaking through, it is always possible to fall back on Anglo-American relations. We at Yeovil are at present formalising this splendid instrument of general dis-ease, gambits, counter gambits, and the one-up-one-down atmosphere. We are rather proud of our name for it—"Manglo-Relations"—which has been formed syncretically from the two terms "Anglo-American Relations" and "mangled feelings." The natural friendliness, the recognition of a home from home, the geniality and mutual admiration which exist between the two nations, can always be frustrated by anyone who uses the word Relations, with its disagreeable double meaning.

This can be brought in indirectly, or insidiously, by expressions based on the phrases students should have memorised from the beginning of this chapter: "The British are our best friends" or "The freedom of the world depends on America and England keeping in close touch, pooling common knowledge and working eye to eye." Whatever phrase you use, the Manglo-Relations Department can always be guaranteed to put temporarily out of joint the firmest and most lasting friendship in the world, and frustrate the un-Lifemanly habit, much in evidence recently between British and Americans, of just plain ordinary liking each other.